Praise for *Your Body Is a Revolution*

"Although it would have been an easier path to instruct us how to be in our bodies in one particular way, Teng does the braver and more skillful thing of calling us to be in relationship with our own bodies, to let our own sensuality light the way to a more liberated future of connection."

—**Dr. Hillary L. McBride**, therapist, author, speaker, podcaster

"This is a book that I highly recommend to anybody searching to decolonize their life through embodiment. It is a must-read to gain the insight and inspiration that's needed in today's world. Having hard conversations is something we need to move forward in a good way as a collective of human beings on Mother Earth."

—**Dakota Bear**, Indigenous rights activist, and cofounder of Decolonial Clothing

"As someone who has religious trauma, nothing has been more transformative for my recovery than learning the language of my body. Our bodies are speaking to us all the time, but too often we dismiss them to our own detriment. In this book, Teng shows us the way to pay attention to our bodies, to trust in them, to fall into our bodies and in love with them. It will change everything."

—**Cindy Wang Brandt**, author of *Parenting Forward* and *You Are Revolutionary*

"As a queer, Black femme, I am struck and impressed by Teng's intentionality in making the reader aware of her own intersections and the ways they inform her work and service to the world. She rejects assumptions and broad statements that often dismiss the experiences of marginalized bodies. This book truly welcomes all bodies to the table to heal and live fully in our truest, most authentic forms."

—**Coach Yeamah**, creator of Confidently Queer

"With authenticity, passion, and conviction, Teng has written a book that both challenges the reader and points them back to their most valuable resource: their body. Teng's work reveals the disservice that has occurred for generations through systems of oppression that have required humankind to live from a space of disconnect from themselves, the collective, and the Earth. Simultaneously, Teng offers hope through education, research, and tangible somatic practices to find a way back to ourselves."

—**Dr. Laura Anderson**, Center for Trauma Resolution and Recovery, and the Religious Trauma Institute

"Reading this book feels like being tenderly coached into a deeper awareness of your body and the stories they have to tell. The earth, and every living body within it, has needed this book to exist for a long time. Teng's willingness to birth this deep wisdom into the world is a powerful gift and one that can profoundly change us all—if we let it."

—**Jamie Lee Finch**, embodiment coach and author of *You Are Your Own*

"Tara Teng is a beautiful voice of both timeless and urgent wisdom. Through her unique life experience, she is able to weave together a number of intersections to help others on the journey of embodiment and self-reclamation come home to their wholeness. Don't just read this book—*experience* this book as a revolution for yourself and as an embodied prayer for all other bodies."

—**Morgan Day Cecil**, creator of The Feminine Wholeness™ Method

"This is a book that will support anyone's journey into breaking generational cycles of disembodiment and disconnection through collective care and reexamination of dehumanization and body-based oppression. Tara Teng provides a comprehensive and compassionate pathway to reconnecting to our own bodies and each other through insightful reflections. By trusting the wisdom embodied within her, she weaves the political and abstract into discernible ways that shift us toward nonviolence. I especially loved the gender-expansive and sexually inclusive ways she challenges us to think about the spiritual and natural world! You need all the support you can get when confronting trauma, and this book is an amazing companion in that journey!"

—**Alma Zaragoza-Petty**, author of *Chingona: Owning Your Inner Badass for Healing and Justice*

"I've seen Tara Teng live out the message of this book over many years to become the fully embodied version of herself. She is an inspiration and a powerful guide and teacher, precisely because she's lived this revolution in her own body. *Viva!*"

—**Idelette McVicker**, author of *Recovering Racists: Dismantling White Supremacy and Reclaiming Our Humanity*

YOUR

BODY IS A
REVOLUTION

YOUR
BODY IS A
REVOLUTION

HEALING OUR RELATIONSHIPS WITH OUR BODIES, EACH OTHER, AND THE EARTH

Tara Teng

Broadleaf Books

Minneapolis

To those who long to feel liberation in their bodies.
May we find our way back home to ourselves
and heal our relationships with each other.

Contents

Introduction

On a warm summer evening in late August, I was wandering the concrete streets of downtown Vancouver, Canada, alongside someone I had just met. The cool air rustled through the trees in one of the world's greenest cities as we passed by the structures of street art and listened to the sounds of cars, distant chatter, street performers, and crosswalk countdowns. As we turned a corner from the financial district toward the entertainment neighborhood, we encountered a male-presenting young person walking down the street wearing a beautiful long, sequined skirt. His style was captivating, and our eyes could not help but lock on him as he walked down Granville Street with such confidence, laughing with his friends flanking him on either side. A hype woman through and through, I cheered him on and called out how amazing his style was. His face lit up with a smile; he tipped his flat-brimmed hat to me and gave his long skirt a swish and a twirl, sending the reflection of a thousand mini disco lights across the concrete pavement.

In this moment, I was watching someone truly living on their own terms and in alignment with their authenticity. This human was another walking embodiment of liberation! I had connected with a kindred spirit who found themselves in a world searching for truth, and I was energized at the sight of him! But the person I was with went rigid in their body, raised an eyebrow, and commented on how the style choice of this male-presenting human was "interesting."

I could hear in their voice the disapproval and disdain. In a previous life, I would have been too shy and afraid of rejection to challenge their reaction. But to protect the radical act of authenticity that I had just witnessed, I summoned my inner mama bear and responded back that I'm always going to cheer for someone who shows up authentically in their full self, reminding the person I was with of how much courage it takes to do that.

I remember the first time I met Tara in all her authenticity, but it was a long journey back to her. I'm sure I knew her in my earliest years, but somewhere along the way, she became lost to me as I absorbed messages from my surroundings that told me I had to behave a certain way, look a certain way, and speak a certain way in order to be accepted, seen, and loved. This indoctrination process began when I was around six years old as a shy, homeschooled half-Asian girl taking cues from my peers in ballet class about how I ought to behave socially. Under the backdrop of floor-to-ceiling studio mirrors, I took notice of which girls were considered the beautiful ones and who was popular and who was not. No one told us about the hierarchical structure that we were about to insert ourselves into, but we filtered ourselves into categories based on what we saw represented in the media and in the world around us, and we learned to behave accordingly. This changed the relationships I had with the other girls in my class, but it changed my relationship with my body as well. With large, unforgiving mirrors reflecting every angle, we learned how to criticize our perceived flaws. Our innocent developing bodies didn't know any better and were simply growing to nourish us and prepare us for the days that lay ahead. But instead of receiving loving words of adoration, our bodies heard verbal abuse, and some may have even experienced self-harm behind the closed doors of our homes.

This self-conscious scrutiny of who I was and where I belonged only deepened in my teenage years as I learned alongside my peers how to flirt with those I was attracted to and absorbed the messages about what the world defines as popular and desirable. I spent these tender years entrenched in evangelical youth group culture, listening to Relient K, playing capture the flag in overgrown forests after the sun had set, and wearing shirts that always covered my shoulders so that I wouldn't be pulled aside to receive a lecture from my youth leader about not causing the boys to stumble. At youth group, at summer camp, and in the hallways at school, our female bodies were constantly measured for modesty and holiness.

As a young adult, I was thrust into the spotlight, wearing a jeweled crown on my head and a sash that bore the name of my country. With all eyes on me, I carried the responsibility to represent not only myself but also my pageant organization and my entire country on the world stage. With this sash came an expectation of who Miss Canada is, and anytime I stepped outside that expectation, the world had something to say about it. There were entire internet forums dedicated to discussing the outfit I had worn each day and whether I lived up to people's expectations. The stress caused me to skip meals. Only one country's representative would come out on top for her ability to embody the ideals of womanhood as objectively defined by our collective societies and ideologies. All of us were trying to obtain an untenable and constantly moving goalpost.

Two days after I crowned my Miss Canada successor, I took on a new title and became a wife, once again stepping into an expectation that had been laid out before me. Twenty-five years of living in the evangelical church, a cultural identity that prides itself on traditional family values, told me what their expectations were of wives for their husbands. I learned to cook for the first time in my life and did my best to be the "good wife" that I had seen exalted as the standard for a good marriage. But five years and two beautiful children later, our marriage came to its end. And this ending was pivotal for me.

The dominant narrative about divorce suggested that this is where my life ended, and in many ways, it was. The woman I had been told to be died the day I left my marriage. But the woman I was born to be had been slowly dying inside each day to make room for the fabricated me to live. Eventually, I couldn't do it anymore. I could no longer sacrifice everything I was born to be for everything I was told to be. Over time, my marriage had become an unsafe situation that wasn't healthy, and no one in our family was happy. I had to let the fabricated versions of us go and grieve their passing.

And so my marriage came to an end and the world as I knew it crumbled. It was devastating. Almost daily, I found myself in the fetal position on my shower floor, weeping every last tear from my body. I sobbed on my therapist's couch and sat on the edge of the ocean's shoreline reading poetry, as if each word could tether me to something concrete that would help me find my way home. For eighteen months after the divorce, I walked through the world trying to keep my head above water. I was in survival mode, trying to keep myself together and my children whole as our world shifted into something new. It was the hardest year and a half of my life.

Then slowly, as the earth's seasons transformed around me, I began to set my feet on steady ground again. And I started an honest conversation with my body about our life, perhaps for the first time ever. Rather than boxing up my emotions and shoving them deep into the back corner of my life's closet, I chose to unpack it all, examining every single piece of baggage that I was hauling around with me through life. I looked at the messages I had absorbed in my childhood about what I needed to do to be loved. I became critical of the pledges I took in my youth that assigned virtue to purity and taught me to appease the powers that be to sustain the hierarchies of tradition. I dismantled the ideas I had been indoctrinated into that dictated what a family looked like and how I ought to relate to those that I loved. And at the center of it all, I deconstructed the fraying tapestry of faith as I knew it, pulling on each string as I followed my hunger for truth and a longing in my heart for something more.

Through it all, my body was with me. Returning home to the relationship with my body that I had once known as a child, I slowly began to build back trust within myself. My closest friend and greatest ally—my body—came back and took her rightful place beside me. The numbness I had been feeling after years of systemic silencing began to dissipate, and every fiber of my being began to wake up again. I learned to cultivate the art of listening to my body, to the still small voice within, and trusting in the goodness within me to lead me back home to where I was meant to be. Eventually, I found embodiment as a spiritual practice. Where fundamentalism taught me to distrust my body, embodiment taught me to find goodness within. No longer did I have to go searching in the halls of academia, retreat centers, or cathedrals to find wisdom and goodness. No longer did I have to cling to what others told me about spirituality; I could discover it for myself. Through reclaiming embodiment, I began to know, deep in my bones, that my body is not inherently evil. Rather, my body can speak to me the mysteries of what it means to be fully human and how I can experience heaven on earth in the here and now. Where I once believed that my body would lead me away from God, I have instead found the truth that my body is the place where I meet God. And that truth has brought me back to life.

Who This Book Is For

This book is for you if you have a body. As we will explore in this book, bodies matter deeply and historically, and we have not given bodies the reverence and understanding they deserve. This book is also for you if you have grown up in the church or lived in a country or culture that has been heavily influenced by the church. At times in this book, I will dissect ideas from theology—not in an effort to convince you of anything but for us to better understand where our cultural ideas come from and how they impact our relationships with our bodies and each other.

The church has given many of us generations of trauma stemming from shame-filled ideology of the body. This can be true even if we never set foot in a church ourselves. Maybe you know firsthand what it feels like to be wounded by the church or to have theology weaponized against you; I certainly do. While I no longer identify as a Christian, I've found Jesus in a new, fresh way, apart from capitalism, patriarchy, colonization, and white supremacy. Many of the clients I work with are survivors of religious trauma, and if this is your story, I want to gently share a trigger warning with you: Parts of this book speak to all the ways that theology and the institution of the church has perpetuated body-based oppression, injustice, and disembodiment. I do not expose this harm in an effort to further villainize or attack religion but rather to explore together the ways we can break cycles of harm and come back into relationships of ethical balance and reciprocity with one another.

Finally, if you have felt disconnected, lost, unsure, unsafe, overwhelmed, or like an imposter in your body, then this book is for you. You no longer need to fit in to be safe, find belonging, or feel loved. Together we will unwind the lies your body has absorbed from patriarchy, colonization, and white supremacy so that you can reclaim your true self in all its powerful authenticity. Maybe you want to meet yourself with full authenticity, but you don't know how because the only narrative you've ever heard is that your body is something that you must sacrifice on the altar in order to prove to God that you are good, holy, and pure. Maybe you were taught that your body is inherently sinful and that listening to your body will lead you down the slippery slope toward an eternity in hell. I want to cordially invite you to leave all that behind.

How to Read This Book

So much awaits you on the other side of toxic, body-shaming narratives. I know because I've been there. I was raised in the same patriarchal, colonized, capitalist society that you were, and I want you to know it is possible to reclaim your body in an expansive way that holds space for all of you. You can leave behind all the lies, all the inner tension and turmoil, all the disconnection that you feel from your own body.

Through my work as a somatic practitioner, I see the world through the lens of the body. Somatics is a field of bodywork that studies and embraces a holistic way of being human, with mind, body, and soul intertwined. With this foundation, I do the gentle work of coming home to the body on a daily basis. If this feels foreign to you, or if you think you are the only one who feels disconnected in your body, I promise: you are not. I have worked with hundreds of people who are doing the courageous work of unlearning all the harmful beliefs they have about their bodies and learning how to be more authentically themselves. This is a powerful act of reclamation and revolution! The systemic structure of the world we live in is optimized for disembodiment, but this is not how it is meant to be. My clients and I get curious about all the ways our bodies speak to us, and how we can unravel the many layers of trauma that our bodies are holding. By speaking truth to limiting beliefs, we can release the grasp that shame has on us and end the ways we are at war with our bodies. Sometimes this looks like talking things out so that we can see them from a new perspective. Sometimes this looks like moving big emotions through our body with the tools of dance or breath work. Other times this looks like an inward self-reflection and embodied conversation with our full selves. All the time, this looks like a brave person doing the tender work of coming home.

But the journey ahead will be difficult. It will force you to examine every belief you hold and get to the source of those beliefs. There may be a grieving process as you let go of what can no longer serve you. There may be moments when you feel alone in the process, or you have to confront traumatic memories that you would rather not acknowledge. You'll likely feel many different emotions and physical sensations while reading. If you can, and if it feels safe enough for you, try to notice what emotions arise and how your body is feeling as you read. There may be moments when you feel inspired, excited, light, powerful, elated, hopeful, and even ecstatic in your body. There may be words that resonate so deeply within you that you feel your very soul reflected to you on the page and the secret longings of your heart whispering to you from within.

You don't need to read the chapters of this book in the order that they are presented. Some chapters may be deeply triggering to you, and if this happens, I invite you to pause or skip over to the next chapter. But when you feel ready, please come back. Our triggers are not places we need to avoid forever; learning to lean into the feelings that arise, when we have support, can be deeply healing and give us the opportunity to rewrite a new story into our nervous system. But if it feels safe enough, I invite you to sit with discomfort. In my coaching practice and somatic therapy sessions, I sit with my clients when this happens. It is through holding space for the uncomfortable or hard emotions that we learn from them and grow our resilience for the hard things that elicit a trigger response in our bodies. I highly recommend seeking out a somatic practitioner or therapist who has an antioppressive and trauma-integrative approach.

I am a bisexual, biracial Asian American, cisgender woman, and my perspective has been shaped by these pieces of who I am. Because

I have grown up in a country that is now part of modern-day colonial North America, I will refer to many of my lived experiences within this cultural context. However, because the human experience is so vast and diverse, I have invited others to join me on this journey, and I share their voices alongside mine in various parts of this book.

As I share stories in this book, I am recalling moments as I know them to be. My retelling of a memory might be different from someone else who also was there. This is because our perspectives, our lived experiences, our trauma, and our biases are all different, so we experience and recall things differently. This context is so incredibly important to the embodied stories and beliefs we hold. In *The Politics of Trauma*, somatic practitioner and trauma researcher Staci Hanes states, "We are shaped by and embody the social condition in which we live." This is incredibly important when we want to heal our broken relationships with our bodies, each other, the earth, and spirituality.

I promise you, the journey is worth it. You are worth it. Where patriarchy, colonization, and white supremacy push for the ideal body, with dominance over others, embodiment is the radical act of resistance in the face of this oppression. We all face significant barriers to achieving such liberation. This begs the question: What would we do today if we weren't so afraid of the confines and backlash created by the status quo? This is why it is entirely captivating to witness humans who live their fullest selves: the ones who are honest about their journey, who do not hide themselves from the world or seek to occupy places that no longer serve them. Throughout this process, I hope you will come to find that your body is a revolution and that showing up in your truest self is a powerful act of resistance to the system that tries to shame us into feeling bad about our bodies. After you have stripped away everyone else's agendas, you'll be left with only your authentic self, and you'll be ready to start rebuilding a worldview in alignment with your values and a relationship with your body that you once knew intimately as a child, before everyone's else ideas about bodies overshadowed your own. That's what I witnessed on the streets of Vancouver as I watched this person twirl with the sparkle of his skirt. And that's what you can witness within yourself when you choose to do the work.

Here I hope you will find answers from deep within, from an embodied place. My job is to help facilitate the relationship between you and your body, first and foremost. But while I may be your embodiment coach, doula, and guide along the way, I want to make it clear: I am not your teacher; your body is your teacher. I am simply the facilitator assisting you as you learn to listen to her/him/them. Your body is the answer, and you already have everything within you that you need. It is my prayer that this book will be the roadmap that whispers hope into the longings of your soul and sets you on a path to freedom and healing.

Finally, if you have someone you can read this book alongside, I encourage you to do so. Transformation comes most powerfully through relationships. Our lives are not meant to be lived alone, and returning to right relationship with our bodies must also include returning to right relationship with one another. So if you can, please read this book alongside a trusted friend who makes you feel safe enough to explore the fullest expression of yourself. Book clubs are an especially sacred space for journeys like the one on which you are about to embark. And if you can't find a friend close to you, I invite you to join the pockets of the digital community that exist in online spaces that allow you to feel fully seen, fully held, and fully embraced. This is what we need to thrive.

This is your invitation to fully inhabit your life. To reclaim what has been stolen from you, to remember the parts of yourself that you have distanced yourself from. To take back what they said was too much, too loud, too feminine, too masculine, too gay, too worldly, too unique to fit into the mold of what patriarchy, colonization, and white supremacy decided was acceptable. This is your invitation to come back home to the place you were always searching for. Here your whole self is welcome. You no longer have to cut off, censor, diminish, or abandon parts of yourself to gain acceptance. Here we embrace wholehearted living. Here we live in alignment with our values and beliefs, not fear-based behavior established by institution-alized control. Here we speak truth to power and dismantle all forms of body-shame oppression and control. Here your body is good and holy, something that brings you closer to goodness, something that invites you into a deeper understanding of what it means to be fully human. Here we call one another into greater life, putting aside what holds us back and knowing that more is always possible.

So welcome home, beloved. We have been waiting for you. The fire is warm, the candles are lit, and the table is set. Let's find our way back together. You are not alone on the journey any longer. You have found your people: the misfits and wanderers, the ones searching for wholeness and truth. We will fill our bellies with good food, our minds with conversation, and our hearts with all the promises of a world longed for, built on justice, liberation, and love for all. You're home, in exactly the skin you're in.

Thank you for trusting me on this journey, dear one. In every word I write, your freedom is on my mind.

With Conviction,

Tara

Chapter 1

Reclamation

Your whole self is welcome here.

"Truth feels like something in the body." I heard my friend, Coach Yeamah, the founder of Confidently Queer, say directly to my soul. I let her words echo for a moment as every cell in my body vibrated with deep resonance to the truth they had just heard. "*Yes,*" my body whispered, as it clung onto each word like a life raft in the midst of a turning ocean. This is exactly the truth that I lead my clients to in every session: *truth feels like something in my body.* It's that jolt of energy that runs through you when someone gives language to something that you've experienced and know to be true. It's a deep sense within you that brings you back into remembering, waking you up again and calling you back.

For a long time, I had been numb to the experience of living in my body. I silenced my body's voice, learning to distrust what she was speaking to me. My relationship with my own body had become clouded by patriarchal forces that infiltrated theology, mass media, culture, my relationships, and my own internalized gaze. Instead of listening to the wisdom from within, I listened to the authoritarian voices over me that said my body would lead me astray, that my body could make another person "stumble," that my body's natural desires were something to shut down and be ashamed of. And so I began to view my body as a stranger rather than an ally, beginning a complicated relationship fraught with internalized misogyny, white supremacy, and the male gaze. I saw my body as something to overcome rather than a relationship to be embraced.

Through my work as an embodiment coach, I've learned that my experience is not uncommon. Every single person I have met so far has a complex relationship with their body. When we seek to heal those relationships, we often end up unraveling all the reasons we are distanced from our bodies in the first place.

All day every day, we exist in our bodies. This is an undeniable fact that we can all agree on and a universal experience we all share. We wake, we eat, we breathe, we feel, and we move. Some of our bodies, like those of professional athletes, deny all logical laws of gravity, flexibility, and strength. Some of us use our bodies to shield the vulnerable by putting ourselves in harm's way to protect them. But even if all we do is deeply breathe the air around us into our lungs, it is our magnificent bodies that allow us to do so. But what is the body? Is it a conglomerate of matter, mass, blood, and bones? Is the body us—the very essence of who we are? And how does the very experience of living in our bodies impact the people we become? These are the questions we will explore together in this book. This is the journey we are on; the journey of being human.

My Inner Child Was Embodied

Viewing the body as a separate and inferior part of us can lead to our disembodiment. We may treat the body as temporary. We may see the body's desires as carnal, sinful, and distracting and shut down the experience of living in our bodies because collectively we have decided that things of the intellect and spirituality are more important. Distrust of the body creates a growing chasm between who we are and how we perceive ourselves, which fosters disintegration within us. We cut off and admonish our body, our sexuality, our hunger, and our desires because someone or society told us it was better if we did so. Falling into this trap is easy to do.

Do you remember the first time that you realized others could perceive you and your body differently than you perceived yourself? I remember the day it happened. I was about five or six years old. I think this was the moment I lost my freedom to fully inhabit my body. I had spent the entire hot summer afternoon playing on my friend's playground in her backyard. As I climbed to the top of the clubhouse, I crouched down and prepared to catapult my body down the slide toward the green bed of lush grass and earth below. But before I did, for a split second my eyes locked eyes with a little neighbor girl on the other side of the fence next door. She wore a pristine sundress and had her hair pulled back neatly into two perfect, blond French braids with ribbons at the bottom of each one. Clutched in her hands, she held a plush teddy bear close. Her eyes looked up at me, wide with amazement.

And as I looked down at her, I caught a glimpse of my shadow, with my wild curly hair falling out of my ponytail in a huge mess around my head. I can't ever be certain what was going on in her mind as we stared back at each other for a short moment that felt like an eternity. She was the perfect image of a clean and tiny little girl, while I looked sweaty and flushed, wild and untamed. While it was only a moment and no words were spoken between us, our exchange lingered with me for a long time afterward. I began to take notice of other little girls around me, how they wore their hair, who looked tidy, and who did not. I wondered what people thought of me at first glance. I started to censor my words, my actions, and my body so I was no longer too wild, too unkempt, or taking up too much space. Suddenly, this carefree nature that would propel my body across the playground with all the strength and energy I could muster was gone.

But at least my body didn't betray me. At least she was still my ally and my friend. I could still depend on her. For the next few years, we traveled through life together as we went to swimming lessons and dance recitals, camping trips and sunny beaches. Then one day, I learned that not only could my body be perceived differently by someone else; it could also be used for someone else because it held a power others wanted or feared. The day I learned that my body could spark arousal in another person was the same day the church taught me to distrust my body.

I must have been around ten or eleven years old, hardly a woman yet, when my world shifted. My friends and I were preparing a dance we had been asked to perform for the Kids Church during that year's Easter Sunday program. We were all the daughters of church leadership, so we had grown up together since we were tiny babies. Now in our preteen years, we found ourselves at church at least three times a week, sometimes more. We led Sunday school classes together, attended youth groups together, and spent our summer at Bible camp together.

That day after our rehearsal, we were all asked by the nice, Christian ladies to gather in one of the Sunday school classrooms, instructed to stand shoulder to shoulder, and then inspected over with the same level of scrutiny that the FBI uses to search a lineup of suspects. The crime in question: *potentially* causing the boys to stumble. Our clothing was looked over from head to toe. They checked to see if our shorts were long enough, our shoulders covered enough, and our dance moves pure enough. And we stood there with bewildered eyes for what felt like an eternity. I remember my body feeling increasingly less safe and more exposed with every passing minute. Inside, I wanted to run. I wanted to be anywhere else but underneath the weight of these examining eyes. Finally, after I stood there, waiting in silence and internally questioning everything from my clothing choices to my intentions to whether or not my own heart was pure, the church ladies came to the conclusion that our wardrobe and dance moves were acceptable to Jesus and safe for the nice church boys too. As always, the comfort of the church boys was prioritized over our emotional safety. While the Easter Sunday program was a success, my relationship with my body was never the same.

What I experienced that day was more than just the policing of clothing. At a deeper level, it was the perpetuation of patriarchy by women who did not even realize they were participating in it. From that day on, all it took was a sideways glance from the church folk or a passive comment in casual conversation and I began to piece together what kind of clothing was acceptable, what kind of body language was considered pure, and what kind of music I was allowed to listen to if I wanted to fit in with the church culture. My indoctrination had begun.

On that day, my world shifted, and my body learned new survival skills as a result. I learned that when I walked with too much sway in my hips, I was too much. If I danced at all, I was too much. If I had something to say that wasn't in line with the approved doctrine, or was too loud, or talked out of turn, I was too much. I learned how to self-police my actions, my voice, and my body so that no one else had to do it for me. I never again wanted to feel as vulnerable as I did when standing in the examination lineup in the Sunday school room. This process of self-censoring was born out of a desire for protection and was my body's way of keeping me safe and away from feelings of shame.

Shame was handed to me by someone else who had made a judgment on my body. By self-censoring to assimilate, prove my goodness, and blend in, I made myself small and was ushered into a ritual of human history. For hundreds of years, people have inspected each other's bodies, categorizing them in societal constructs to determine what is and isn't acceptable by the status quo.

Systemic Disembodiment

Gatekeeping these social constructs in the name of morality or "traditional values" is one of the things that the church has become known for. And we don't have to be part of the church to have been influenced by it. For women, this has looked like the medieval practice of dunking. Women who were accused of being witches had rocks tied to them as they were tossed into the river, proven innocent if they could not use their feminine powers of magic to save them (but dying in the process) and guilty if they could. In 1692, this looked like the Salem Witch Trials, when young girls turned on women in the community and two hundred people were accused of witchcraft, resulting in the death of a number of people. The church oversaw many of these trials and reinforced the hierarchy of traditional gender roles, solidifying a distrust of anyone who was other in the name of morality. During this time, vast amounts of earth-based wisdom were lost, and the relationship with the earth that many people held as sacred was severed. Much of this gatekeeping was rooted in Euro-centric Western culture, where white, cisgender, heterosexual, Anglo-Saxon Protestant males held the governing authority and upheld ideology that viewed everyone else as a threat. Through these witch trials, violence and terror were strategically used to force all other embodied expressions of our humanity into submission and hiding. Today, there is so much intergenerational trauma running through our blood. We no longer burn women or queer people at the stake; instead, through community policing and self-sacrifice, we simply hand each other the matches to slowly light ourselves on fire.

For men, this process throughout history has been a more subtle form of violence, and the self-policing from within the community still remains. Over the years, the confines of patriarchy have shifted the goalposts of what it means to be a man, with ancient Greek men able to take on same-sex lovers without question of their manliness and Elizabethan men able to perform female-presenting characters in costume—two actions that would not have been acceptable practice by "manly" men in North America during the 1940s or 1950s. Yet while perceived manliness has seen more ebb and flow than perceived femininity, the overall ideals of strength, bravery, and protection have remained tied to the idealized version of masculinity throughout much of human history. And while men have enjoyed more freedom of expression than women, the measurement of who they are tends very much to be calculated by their performance of strength, an oppression in and of itself.

The process of colonization has largely erased the existence of humans who live beyond the gender binary. Yet Two-Spirit people exist all across Turtle Island, and prior to colonization, they were revered as respected community leaders, often taking on the roles of healers, matchmakers, counselors, and more. Two-Spirit and gender-nonconforming people invite us into more expansive possibility for the human experience, something we'll dive deeper into in chapter 7.

With these very real threats of violence, we have learned throughout history to self-police our behavior, our words, our expression, our sexuality, and our bodies as an act of survival. It is our body's response to the threat of danger, perceived or real, and much of our body's fight-or-flight response has been initiated by the intergenerational trauma that we have inherited from our ancestors who lived through the oppressions listed previously and more. Through this process, we become disembodied, separating ourselves from the rawness of our human authenticity, because the truth of who we are is deemed "too much" for the status quo and the powers that be. Our bodies, which were initially meant to be our greatest allies in life, become our biggest threat, so we silence them in an attempt to be safe. This separation of self creates a complex relationship with our bodies, in which we distance ourselves from our authenticity as an act of survival.

In the Name of God

I will never get over the ways that body-based oppression and terrorism stemming from patriarchy, colonization, and white supremacy were often done in the name of God. This toxic theology stems from an ideology that our bodies will lead us to sin. Guided by this ideology, we fear the possibilities of the body and seek to control them, to establish dominance over the body, and because of our racist history of colonization and patriarchy, we learn to fear those who live in bodies beyond the default of white, slender, athletic, able, and youthful. We must unravel each of these internalized messages we hold and trace them back to their origins, as they impact our intergenerational lineage from ancient history to today.

With this in mind we can examine how white-dominated spaces have become the most prominent within the Western world, and how the Western world is most dominant on the global stage. By following this thread of history, we see the impacts of colonization, the heinous crimes of slavery, and the oppression of misogyny, all often perpetuated through the reach of the church. It's a harsh reality to face, but if we are to find our way back to our bodies and each other, we must critically examine the impact that the church and other institutions have historically had on the Western world. We must look at how our understandings of the body are shaped through a lens of scripture that has been wielded as a weapon against our bodies, disconnecting us from God, ourselves, the earth, and each other.

Because of Christianity's political dominance over the world, all history has been influenced by church history, and what we believe about the body goes back to our theology. As someone who grew up in the church, I was raised on countless sermons on how we ought to deny our flesh and set our eyes on the things of heaven. I endured even more sermons that preached about resisting temptations and our human propensity to fail. I was raised in a community that believed in "sin nature theology": that sin is in our human nature, that we are unable to resist temptation, and that we are inherently bad and desperately wicked in our bodies from the moment we are born. I was taught to "flee from sexual immorality" and presented a hierarchy of sins, with all carnal desires labeled the worst.

In response, I learned to "put on the full armor of God" and built walls around myself that disconnected me from intimacy with my body. Like the rest of my generation and the ones that came before me, I internalized every message that taught me to distrust my body, believing that my body was going to lead me astray from God and in my efforts to be faithful, I became more and more disembodied and disconnected from the skin I was born in. This is not a new phenomenon. We read in 1 Corinthians 9:27 that Paul would discipline, strike, and pummel his body to keep it under control, passing on a theology that perpetuates the belief that the body is something to silence and overcome. As a result, the church continued to preach disembodiment, prioritizing the importance of the intellect and the spiritual over the body. These ideas permeated the church, and because of the ways the church was enmeshed with state power, those ideas influenced the wider society as well. All the while, none of these ideas were shared by the central figure of the Christian faith, Jesus Christ.

Jesus wasn't asking us to deny our bodies to be more spiritual. If anything, we can look to his life to see how he embraced his body by living with and among the people, by breaking bread and sharing meals in community, by washing feet in service and allowing himself to be touched by others who reached out for him. Jesus got close to the bodies of others. He was not afraid of his humanity. When Jesus reached out to touch the man with leprosy, he didn't flinch. He didn't pull back. He was not seeking to separate himself from human experience but rather showed us that we can find God in the midst of our human experience—making our whole lives holy.

The Complexity of Being Human

The body shows me that being human is good. And at the same time, it cannot be denied that the human experience knows goodness as well as hardship. We all know the depth of heartbreak and betrayal. I have agonized in the weight of pain from my own brokenness or someone else's malice toward me. I have wept desperate tears of misery until my very soul felt empty. So it would be incomplete to say that our human experience is only good. We all have felt suffering enough to know this is not true. And so this here is the paradox of being human: we are more than one thing at the same time. We are inherently good and yet broken and capable of inflicting so much pain.

I invite you to reimagine what life could look like if you were no longer afraid to embody the fullness of who you are. I invite you to taste what it feels like to live with such unapologetic abandon of the expectations and perception of others. I invite you to prioritize loyalty to the pure embodiment of your authentic self—it will not lead you astray. I invite you to heal the trauma that lives in your body by going back for your inner child that you've tried to keep safe. I invite you to begin a conversation with your body and reimagine what it could look like if you came back into right relationship with all things. It would be revolutionary. Maybe you will find that all the answers lie in your body and you'll learn how to find your way back to truth on your own. The systems, ideologies, and institutions built on hierarchies of body-based oppression would shake at their core if we were to cast aside all the societal pressure from their manipulation and lies about our bodies and our relationships with one another. This is how embodiment can lead us home and back to one another again. May the revolution begin.

Reflection

* How has your relationship with your body changed through your lifetime? How would you describe your relationship with your body as it is now? What has brought you to this point?
* What would you like your relationship with your body to look like? Imagine how that might feel in your body.

Invitation

Find a comfortable place where you can be with your body, free of distractions. Find a comfortable position to sit, stand, or lie down in. Follow the guide of your body. Connect to your body through breath, movement, stillness, song, or voice—whatever is meaningful to you. When you feel grounded in the moment and connected to your body, ask your body, "What do you need from me?"

Every great relationship begins with communication, listening, and reciprocity.

This is where we begin.

Chapter 2

Shaking Off Shame

Your body is good. Deeply and wholly good. Eternally good. Period. Anyone or anything that tells you otherwise likely has a political agenda or power to gain over you. Don't listen to them.

Have you ever watched a baby discover their toes for the first time? In the early days of motherhood, I would watch my babies play with their toes all day long—truthfully, sometimes I still go through my entire camera roll on my phone just so I can relive their baby days again! There's something so pure and precious about these early days of discovery. Babies look at their feet with wonder and amazement. They wiggle each toe in exploration, discovering what it can do. They pull their toes up to their face to taste them and grasp the feel of their foot in their chubby little hands, curious about what they will do with these toes and how these toes will impact their day.

Waking up to our embodiment can make us feel like an infant discovering we have toes for the first time. It can be awe-inspiring to realize that not only do we have a body to live in and navigate the world through but that our body can speak to us, share wisdom with us, and hold memories for us. Our body can be a powerful resistance to the status quo that seeks to harness the goodness of our body for the gain of profit or power.

Our bodies are both the great equalizer—as we all experience life in a body—and the source of our division, as our diverse bodies allow us each to experience life differently. We all bleed in the same way. But differences in how our bodies look, move, navigate the world, and have needs can cause division and even hate among us. Our body differences create categories and communities that, at their best, foster a sense of belonging and understanding. At their worst, these categories and communities breed into a pyramid of power hierarchies based on skin color, age, sex, gender, ability, and more. As a result, the body is a complex, wonderful, and sometimes painful place to live. But what is the human experience at its core? Are we a body? Or are we a soul? Or maybe we are something more entirely? Our bodies go through every aspect of life with us because *they are us*. When we view our bodies as bad, it reflects a belief that we, as a living being, are bad. This ideology can break our relationships with our bodies. The shame cycle builds when we punish and deny our bodies, judging them for doing the very thing they are designed to do: live.

Living into the fullness and the complexity of this paradox is where we find our freedom. My earliest memory of feeling this freedom in presence was when I was around ten or eleven years old, attending church camp and sneaking off to the creek, away from the noise of crowds and closer to the trees. I would walk down the trail, past the decrepit old wooden A-frame chapel that had become reclaimed by the forest, and down a steep winding trail toward the rushing creek. I would lay down with my back upon the tiny one-person dock, with my neck leaned all the way back so I could submerge my hair into the cool water. Feeling supported by the wooden

beams beneath me, I would let my long, wild curls dance in the bubbling current of the creek. No one else in the world knew where I
was, but Spirit was there with me, playing with my hair as it spun
along the bubbles of the rushing creek. Here, I could let go. I could
relax into the movement of the water as I looked up at the strong
branches of cedar swaying overhead. I could breathe. The underlying tension that I held in my body from being a pastor's daughter in
a small town and everyone's expectation on me began to melt away.
Comments I had heard about bodies, sexuality, social class, or political alignment drifted down the creek, away from me, and I was left
with the freedom to simply be in my body. I no longer had to live in
my head thinking about my body; instead, I could experience everything through my body. Fully present. Birds sang, and I was left with
the communion of Spirit all around me.

In that moment, nature preached to me a sermon of finding
goodness in all things; the changing leaves of the maple tree could
mirror to me lessons of letting go, and the constant movement of
the creek could remind me of how if we are stagnant, we are denying our purpose. Every bit of the natural world was a tiny lesson if I
was willing to stop and listen. And through those moments, Spirit,
the energetic presence that can be felt when we are connected to
the Source of all things, was closer to me than ever—a peace that
surpassed all understanding. For many years after, I would try to
re-create that feeling through meditation, reimagining myself back
on that little dock, interconnected with everything around me. But
even as doctrine and church community tried to show me the "right
way" to meet God, I found more divinity in that little creek in the
forest, always calling me back. That little dock on the edge of the
waters taught me to listen and that God could also be found outside
of our religious ideology, in the natural world around us, and in our
very bodies.

Sin Nature Theology and Shame

A few years ago, my son and I were looking at a science book in our home library and on one of the pages was an image of a DNA double helix. I read the words on the pages and began to nerd out about all the intelligent things that the body does and how our DNA makes up the foundation of our bodies. I told him excitedly that he has DNA in his body as well. With heaviness, he turned his little face toward mine and told me in a small voice, "Yes, Mama. But mine is bad." I looked into his big brown eyes and asked with great confusion what he meant by that. He proceeded to tell me that his Sunday school teacher had explained to him that all people, even him, were inherently sinful and that the propensity to sin was embedded into our DNA as humans. She taught this lesson to him with the intention of explaining why humans are in need of a savior. But instead of giving him hope, she had given him body shame and a fear that he was evil at his core. I never let him return to Sunday school after that. Neither adults nor children need to hear that message.

When we view the body as inherently evil and create a structure of rules to protect ourselves from the body, we disassociate ourselves from our bodies and the inherent goodness that they hold. When we believe theology that tells us we are desperately wicked, wretched beings in need of a savior, we push parts of ourselves aside in shame, self-loathing, and discomfort. This shame and self-rejection create disconnection, disassociation, and disembodiment from ourselves and each other. We lose ourselves to the fear of making a mistake rather than accepting that the human experience is an ebb and flow of living in our goodness, occasionally making mistakes but choosing to learn from them in a way that makes us better people in the end. These ideas of a wretched humanity come from the concept of "sin nature theology," the belief that sin is in our nature and that we cannot escape it without the redemption of Jesus. Looking beyond the church, the concept of Pandora's box in Greek mythology describes how evil entered the world, plaguing humanity since the beginning of time.

So instead of buying into the concept of sin nature theology, I now believe that we are inherently good as humans rather than inherently bad. Instead of berating our bodies to absolve ourselves of sin, we can step into a deeper meaning with our lives by building a foundation of reciprocity and right relationship with all things. Instead of digesting shame, we can choose love over hate and right ethical decisions over selfish desires so that we may bring life and abundance rather than death and destruction.

Mind-Body Dualism in Western Culture

The belief that the flesh of our body is wicked is not unique to the church but has poured over and influenced mainstream culture throughout the ages. Often referenced as Cartesian dualism, this belief was widely advocated for by the seventeenth-century French philosopher and mathematician René Descartes. As a result, we call the body's flesh "carnal" and view it with a negative connotation.

We've also seen the ways that Western culture defines the mind and body as separate entities, prioritizing intellect over the body. But this is exactly where we go wrong. We cannot become more holy by denying our humanness. Yet even today, we often reference "mind over matter" and prioritize things of spirituality and mind over the experience of the body. When we go all the way back into the Western historical written record, we see the Hellenistic philosophers beginning to form a mind-body dualism within Greek culture, prioritizing intellect and viewing things of the body as carnal, lowly desires. We see how Plato and Pythagoras both reference *soma sema,* translated as "body equals tomb." This is an idea that they absorbed from ancient Pharaonic mysticism, which saw the body as a prison for the mind and something that humans needed to be freed from. The early writers of the Bible were also heavily influenced by these ideas, building on them in the scriptures, which refer to the heart and body as "desperately wicked" (Jeremiah 17:9). As a young child, I was given this verse to memorize, repeating over and over that "the heart is desperately wicked and deceitful." I was taught to recite it in Sunday school and made to write it over and over while homeschooling at the kitchen table until my cursive was aesthetically pleasing, but on the inside, my body heard these words and began to disassociate and tense at the thought that the very core of who I am is something wicked. This is how complex trauma begins, making us feel disconnected from ourselves and each other. As Hungarian Canadian medical physician and trauma specialist Gabor Maté, MD, shares, "Trauma is not what happened to you. It is what happened inside of you when what happened to you was happening."

Through my work, I come across many others with complex trauma, religious trauma, and systemic trauma from social inequalities and adverse childhood experiences (ACEs). In this role, I am a sacred space holder for clients as they weep before me, feeling deep grief for the damage that was done to them when they were taught to distance themselves from their bodies, cutting them off from their emotions in an effort to stop feeling pain, and viewing their bodies as something that was going to lead them away from goodness and was, instead, something to fear.

In this worldview, we attempt to distance ourselves from our bodies and intellectualize our human experience rather than feeling it and living it. We silence the body's ancestral wisdom by gaslighting ourselves into believing that what we feel is often "all in our heads." Western thought and medicine are all built on this idea that the mind and body are separate as well as the idea of the individual being separate from the collective. Splitting the mind and body results in a culture that teaches us to distance ourselves from the wisdom of the body and from empathy for each other. We view the body as a "meat suit" that we walk around in—something that functionally gets us from place to place, performing daily tasks without much thought to what happens to our bodies and how each daily experience impacts our personhood through our bodies.

But our bodies don't just allow us to move through the world. Our bodies feel, hear, and experience everything we do in this life. Your body is not just part of you; it is you. Everything you have ever been through in life, the highs and the lows: your body experienced it right alongside you. From a neurobiological perspective, when you feel stressed from a tense situation with a work project or a disagreement in a personal relationship, your body also feels it, as a rush of cortisol surges through your veins. When you feel ooey, gooey, mushy, warm fuzzy feelings in the arms of a loved one, that's oxytocin rushing through your veins. When your stomach drops from a trigger of fear or anxiety, that's your body's fight-or-flight response activated in your nervous system, preparing you to fight and survive. These responses are activated in your body through every experience you encounter in a day: through the words your body hears, the physical pain of stubbing your toe or the jerk driver who cut you off on the road. Your body experiences it all and holds on to every single one of these experiences as a memory.

When we understand this process and how our bodies function to protect us from all the experiences we encounter in a day, we can support our bodies better. Our bodies are not trying to betray us when our stomach is twisting in knots; our nervous systems are simply trying to keep us alive by letting us know that something is wrong. These responses are the biological connection to our feelings.

Having compassion for our bodies, holding them tenderly and giving them space to express can soothe our nervous system toward healing. When you do this for yourself, you make a revolutionary act of rehumanizing your body in defiance of every systemic ideology or religious doctrine that taught you to hate your body for simply existing.

For many cultures in the global South, the cultural narrative of mind-body-spirit separation is not mainstream. Indigenous cultures the world over have a deep knowledge of our whole personhood as interconnected and interdependent. We do not exist in isolation but rather, the quality of health and happiness that we experience in this lifetime depends on living in right relationship with all things: with self, with each other, with Spirit, and with the earth. We see this in Taoist beliefs, Tantric practices, and many other Indigenous or Eastern world religions. There is a connection to all things and a remembrance of the fact that we belong to one another. We come from the earth, and we return to the earth. While these words are written in the Christian Bible as well, we tend to focus on the verses of exercising dominion over the earth from a place of power and authority rather than a place of stewardship and communion.

This communion, what Robin Wall Kimmerer in her book *Braiding Sweetgrass* calls "a covenant of reciprocity," is the core of embodiment and justice; it is the way that we return home to our true selves. I am whole, a multilayered and multifaceted individual of mind, body, and soul, but I am also one part of an interconnected web, woven together with everyone else. Everything I do impacts those around me, and everything they do impacts me as well. This covenant, a binding agreement designed for the mutual flourishing of all things, ties our interdependence on one another forever. We—*all of us*—the people, the land, the flora, and the fauna are united in an interconnected way of living with one another. This building of relationships is a spiritual practice of metaphorically setting the table and inviting one another in, into right relationship. It is making more room. It is widening the circle so that everyone has a place of belonging—because inherently we all belong together. And that can only be done when we recognize that our human experience includes mind, body, and soul and that we are more than just an individual; we are part of the collective in communion with earth, each other, and divinity.

If you have been plagued by the shame-filled belief that your body is bad, please read this as your permission slip to leave that incorrect theology behind. There is divinity and goodness within you. You don't have to look anywhere outside of yourself to find it. Slow down and breathe in your human goodness as the air fills your lungs. Remember that you are here and living an embodiment that can connect you to right relationship with it all.

Reflection

* Do you remember a time when you were made to believe that your body was bad, or that you were bad? Where did this belief come from?
* How does this belief show up in your life?
* How does this belief feel in your body?
* Has there ever been a time when you've felt liberated in your spirituality and in your body at the same time? What does that look like to you?

Invitation

If you have struggled under the toxic belief of body-shaming ideologies, write down the lies of negative self-talk that replay in your head. Once you have it down on paper, take a moment to release each criticism out of your body. After you have exposed each lie and limiting belief for what it is, take the paper in your hands and crumple it, safely burn it, or rip it up into little pieces. Witnessing the dissolving of these lies can somatically help your body let go of them as well. You do not need to carry around the self-judgment any longer. It's time to let that go.

Chapter 3

Emotional Expression, Not Repression

Emotions are the way our bodies speak to us, a reflection of our lived experience in this world.

Let's begin this chapter with an embodiment exercise. If it feels safe enough, I invite you to slow your breathing, even take a few moments to set this book aside as you take a moment to be back in your body. As you count to four, allow yourself to take a big, deep breath that fills your belly as it goes soft, round, and full. Hold it there for a moment, then release in four slow counts. Repeat as many times as it takes to feel complete with this pattern.

While you do this, take notice of what's happening in your body as you breathe. A common misconception about embodiment work is that it is the same as meditation or that it's about finding calm, quiet, and stillness. But in embodiment we are not trying to empty the mind or bring stillness; we are trying to notice what is happening within us and allow that self-reflection to provide us with insight into how our bodies are functioning at any given moment, what emotions are living inside the body, where our tender parts are holding on to the wounds of trauma, and how to work with the body for healing and wholeness. We are returning to authenticity and creating space so that we can live our fullest selves without hiding or shame. So as you breathe, notice the sensations that rise within you as you scan your body with each breath, starting at the top of your head and slowly working your way down all the way to your toes.

How do you physically feel in your head?
The muscles in your face?
Your shoulders and your neck?
Do you feel tension anywhere?
Tightening? Heaviness? Tingling?

Sensations are one of the ways the body speaks to us, but oftentimes we push these signals aside until we can no longer hear what our body is saying to us. With subtle nudges, the body uses sensations, emotions, and sometimes illness to tell us that something is wrong. For example, have you ever been in conflict with another human? Have you ever found yourself working in the wrong job? Or the wrong relationship? How does it feel in your nervous system? Our bodies will always tell us when something is not right. Learning to notice what is happening within our own emotional spectrum at any given moment is a very important somatic skill. Listening to our body from an embodied place gives us clues to how our body is processing the information it is picking up from our environment around us. This is called tracking. It's a form of somatic literacy, and it's a powerful skill for us to develop. When we realize that our emotional pulse is constantly changing, we can begin to discern the differences as they are felt within us. Having somatic literacy for the different sensations allows us to become familiar with the feelings of each emotion and helps us discern how anger feels, how jealousy feels, how grief feels, and so on. This familiarity builds the skill of somatic mapping, which makes it more accessible for us to learn to embody our emotions in a healthy way rather than suppress and entrap.

These sensations can be subtly different, but the more we take time to slow down and notice what is happening in our bodies, the better attuned we will be to what our bodies are speaking to us. Like we explored in the last chapter, our bodies experience everything we do. Our bodies are not just part of us; they are us. We cannot be separated. But what happens to our emotions when we shut them down? We can get stuck in the process of our nervous system activation when our bodies begin to respond emotionally to stimuli, and we abruptly shut the process down. Like a record player with a scratch on it, we are unable to complete the process and sing our songs again. According to Dr. Bradley Nelson in the *Emotion Code*, they become trapped inside our bodies and begin to manifest as stress, tension, and disease.

Through the understanding of somatics, we know that emotions are a chemical experience that your body goes through. When this experience gets shut down and is not allowed to make its full circular process through the body, it becomes stuck, as the chemical release and energetic vibration from that emotion have nowhere to go. This is incredibly important information that we all should be taught in basic science class but instead, the wisdom of our bodies remains largely unknown to us. Often we are raised to believe that maintaining social graces means hiding our emotions away because it is not polite or professional to express big feelings in a social setting. As a result, emotions get stuck inside our bodies.

In modern Western culture, we don't consider it polite or professional to show emotion, and being "overly emotional" is usually viewed as a negative characteristic. The first thing we teach children about their emotions is to shut them down. *Shhhhh. Shhhh. Shhhh. Don't cry. Hold it in. Be quiet. Don't be too loud. Don't be too much.*

Don't take up too much space. Don't be an inconvenience. At the first cry, we shush our babies and begin to silence human expression. Likely every parent has felt this societal pressure to keep their babies calm while maintaining composure themselves. When my own children were young, I would put myself into a state of postpartum anxiety while trying to keep my babies behaving "good" while in public. Truthfully, it made grocery shopping, sitting in church, and the worst—traveling on airplanes—intensely stressful because each situation would turn my baby with delicious chubby rolls into a ticking time bomb that could explode with unwelcome emotion at any moment. Toddlers and infants don't care about social graces—they haven't yet been taught how to succumb to social pressure. Toddlers and infants are purely human in their most raw, authentic form. But through the process of socializing children into our society, we often begin disembodying them without realizing it. We disconnect them from the innate wisdom of their bodies by shutting down their expression through emotions.

Yet I find that children are more embodied and in touch with their humanity than adults are. They can release their pent-up emotions in a temper tantrum and go back to being a happy child only five minutes later. Their ability to freely express themselves can be triggering to those of us who have forgotten how to do so. It touches something within us that we ourselves have silenced. I see this often with my clients who come to me unable to express their emotions in adulthood, because as children, their parents didn't know how to sit with them and help them process their complex emotions. Parents taught them to be seen and not heard, to distance themselves from their bodies and shut the emotions down. Because that's what they were taught to do, the cycle of intergenerational trauma continues.

If we lived in very strict homes where our emotions were not welcomed or understood, these messages have been deeply reinforced and have created pathways of disconnection (read: trauma) in our bodies. Strict households may have taught us that expressing our emotions as young children would be met with physical punishment or a lack of emotional care from our primary caregivers. Some parents respond to their children's emotions by pulling back on their emotional care or by trying to get the child to self-regulate before they are developmentally ready for that skill.

If a child displays emotions and then receives corporal punishment from a parent or caregiver, this will often send the message to the child that their emotions are bad. In my coaching practice, I have witnessed how these children grow up to become adults who are unable to express their emotions or access emotional intimacy with others. Undoing the trauma of such an experience and learning to expand our window of tolerance so that we can hold space for big, complex emotions is work that I do with many of my clients. Together we will listen to their body and learn how to process their big emotions by feeling them without labeling them as bad or themselves as bad for having them. It is key that we create a space of trust so that we can feel safe enough to allow those emotions to release. If we do not feel safe with our emotions, then we will learn to fear them.

Being resistant to our emotions leads us to put up walls around our hearts to keep ourselves from feeling big things that we've become uncomfortable with. I understand that feeling is painful sometimes. And if we haven't learned the skills to feel safe expressing our emotions, then letting go of our tightly bound emotions can feel like uncharted territory. We don't know what's on the other side, and many of my clients have expressed a fear of feeling emotions because they worry that if they begin to allow the emotions to roll in, the waves might crash over them like a tsunami. Many of my clients don't know how to process the emotions once it starts, and they fear letting big emotions in means that they will be trapped under the weight of that emotion forever. This is a common result of living in a society that never taught us how to have a healthy expression of our emotions. But if we learn to trust our bodies again—to feel safe in our bodies again and to give our bodies the space to process big emotions—we will eventually discover that our bodies are inherently wise and once we get out of our own way, our bodies know where to take it from there. For many of my clients this looks like sitting with the discomfort of tears, a lump in their throats, or a disassociation with their bodies until we can slowly allow those feelings to come back.

Learning to feel safe with our emotions builds new pathways of connection in our bodies and our brains—helping us reclaim the parts of our humanity that we lost when we shut ourselves down. This is healing for us not only emotionally but physically as well. A 2013 study found that men who suppress their emotions are at great risk of developing cardiovascular disease and an increased risk of cancer mortality. This study linked the disembodiment of emotions to the development of chronic disease and offered further proof that the negative impacts of holding in or avoiding distressing emotions or lacking conscious awareness of our emotions can lead to an early death. And that's just on the individual level as we reflect on our personal relationships with our bodies and our emotions. Ask anyone who has had a parent, friend, or spouse with an immature under-standing of their emotions, and I'm sure they will tell you that sup-pressing emotions doesn't only hurt us personally; it always creates major problems in our ability to nurture deep intimate relationships with others as well.

Misdiagnosis and Misogyny of Emotions

Many of our relationships were broken due to a long history of social isolation inflicted on those whom Western society deems "crazy" or "hysterical." In many places today, we are still forming a culture that has more understanding of mental health needs and the importance of emotions. The medical term *hysteria* has long been misunderstood and used to justify incredible injustices on fellow humans. The root word of *hysteria* stems from the Greek word *hystera*, meaning "uterus." Early Greek ideas on hysteria sparked a widely held belief that abnormalities in the womb could cause physiological problems. This was the explanation of why women are more emotional than men. Many years later, Western medicine still contended that the uterus could wander throughout the body, putting pressure on other organs, which would lead to physical ailment or psychological hysteria.

Until 1980, hysteria was considered a medical condition that predominantly afflicted women and caused psychological problems. This became the default answer that a male-dominated medical industry used to explain the mysterious female body—something that even today causes those who were assigned female at birth to experience lack of competent medical understanding and diagnosis. It is important to note that there is a lack of documentation for the experiences of women of color, making it hard to definitively know how these ideals of medicine and mental health impacted women who weren't white, as we tend to view the past through a white lens. However, what we know is that hysteria became the common diagnosis for the mysterious female body, as doctors labeled women crazy rather than offering proper health care.

In the mid- to late 1800s, insane asylums became the solution for hysteria and the catchall facilities for Victorian women who didn't fall in line with the patriarchal status quo. While looking at the intake documents from many of the facilities across North America, we see that women were institutionalized due to "insanity" for numerous reasons: monthly menstruation or lack of monthly menstruation; overexertion (usually diagnosed in women with seven or more children); childbirth; loss of property; or depression due to the death of a loved one. Enjoying sex or embracing your sexuality could also result in being diagnosed as a nymphomaniac and institutionalized as well. No wonder there is so much stigma around female sexual expression and lack of education of women's sexual pleasure!

Looking at the lack of autonomy women had in the 1800s and 1900s, I see many legitimate reasons for women to be angry. But what I find particularly interesting are intake documents that cite women holding their own ideas on religious matters, experiencing an abusive, violent, or controlling marriage, or reading too many books as the reasons for institutionalization. Through all this documentation, we see that Victorian society had a very narrow view of what a woman should be: quiet, submissive, dutiful, domestic, and maternal. Any woman who held her own ideas, sought bodily autonomy, or used her voice to speak up against gender-based oppression was seen as insane and dangerous and as needing to be locked up and isolated from society.

We may no longer institutionalize women who express their emotions, but the impact of this era of institutionalization still lives in our bones. We fear being "too emotional" because, historically, expressing our emotions has left us unsafe. So we silence ourselves, we take up less space, abandon our own boundaries and we play things off as "no big deal" when really, we feel hurt, violated, or angry because of the actions and choices of someone else. Because hysteria has been seen as a uniquely female ailment, much of our culture still views emotions as effeminate. Due to misogyny, people who freely express their emotions are perceived as weak; this affects people of all genders and ethnic backgrounds.

The Impact of Repressing Emotions

Since the onset of Western colonialism, those assigned male at birth have learned that in order to be perceived as a strong, masculine individual, they must not show weakness. These early colonial ideals were reinforced by many cultural influences of the 1800s and 1900s, most prolifically by the church. Thomas Hugh, an English lawyer, politician, and author wrote *The Manliness of Christ* in an attempt to revive a "muscular Christianity." As we've already explored, these ideals seeped into secular culture as well. The original purpose of the Boy Scouts was to build an "independent manhood" and "make big men out of little boys," according to the organization's historical pamphlets. Due to generations of social conditioning, these patriarchal ideals run deep in our psyches, and our bodies have adapted as a result. Today, societal pressure to "be a man" or "man up" continues, and many boys are given tests of manliness by their peers and parents. Many men seek to protect their sons by "toughening them up" and enforcing the idea that showing emotion equals showing weakness. I've witnessed fathers who mock and dismiss the emotions of sons who are mere toddlers.

Bullying from a parent feels cruel, and it is. Yet through a trauma-informed lens, I try to believe this harsh form of parenting comes from a protective place. If male role models such as fathers and coaches were taunted for not being "manly enough" in their own youth, then it is likely they will pass on that trauma by putting male youth through the wringer as well. Other times, men will seek to protect their children from the mockery of their peers by first toughening it out of them at home, believing they can protect them from the public shame, ridicule, and social isolation they might experience when they get to school. As a result, young boys learn to lock down their emotions and distance themselves from feeling and the cycle of shame continues. As a result, the social landscape that we've all been born into is incredibly hostile to our emotions.

To keep ourselves physically and emotionally safe, we assimilate. We blend in. We shut down our emotions and we seek not to stand out from the crowd. Stoicism and cultural assimilation have become the way. Over time, this way of repressing emotions becomes the cultural norm, as individuals pass on these behaviors to their children, who pass it on to their children, and so on. This is how intergenerational trauma continues to manifest in our bones and our bodies through adapted behaviors. In many cultures, including modern-day North America, stoicism is prized, and disconnection from our bodies is rewarded. A study of the impacts of trauma on the sperm of traumatized rats found that when repeatedly exposed to distressing situations, behavioral and metabolic alterations occur, both in male and female rats, and were passed on to their offspring. Even if their offspring never experienced the trauma themselves, they still responded in the same way that their parents and even grandparents did.

Growing up as a mixed Asian American, I saw this stoicism often. My Chinese Singaporean grandparents were never ones to express their emotions or affections publicly. Hugs, kisses, tears, or exuberant joy were not things that were typically displayed. And yet I knew deeply that I was loved by them. Rather than smothering us with kisses, they doted on us grandchildren by spending hours cooking elaborate meals in the kitchen or bestowing gifts of toys, clothes, and special trinkets sent over from our family still living in Southeast Asia.

While there is nothing wrong with this stoicism, it can be a limiting behavior as well; we don't want to inconvenience others with our pain or to lose face, so we learn to "swallow our pain." This was a phrase I heard often as a child. As Asians, we are raised to be too proud to allow our emotions to leak out and be displayed before others. Some Western cultures are very similar. The British are raised to "keep calm and carry on." North Americans are raised to hide their emotions because it's not good manners to "break down" in front of others. What messages do our bodies receive from this kind of social conditioning? It is no wonder we are locked up, disconnected, and disembodied—it is the only way we know. With Western culture's stigmas around mental health and the long-standing history of social isolation and intergenerational trauma, it's really no wonder that we fear our emotions so greatly. But the truth is that if we want to heal, we must first remember how to feel.

Righteous Anger

If we are searching for personal liberation, we must also look for the ways that our liberation is collectively tied to one another, even in how we experience and express our emotions. One of the ways this has shown up in my life is through my relationship with anger. Anger and I have had a close connection for many years. While most of us are taught to control our anger, I have found that leaning in to understand my anger is much more productive than simply trying to control, push down, and silence it. We tend to perceive anger as something that we ought to diminish, yet there are many circumstances when anger is the appropriate emotion. In order to alchemize anger in an ethical and productive way, we must first build a new relationship with it, one that has respect and reverence as its foundation. If we unleash our anger carelessly and without taking the time to understand it, we will burn everyone in our paths, including ourselves. However, if we slow down and listen to what anger has to say, we can develop a more mature emotional intelligence to help us navigate complex situations of injustice with more humanity. We can still be kind and good even while validating our anger.

When anger shows us injustice, it can be a precious gift. Anger notices whenever the bonds of right relationship are broken. Anger rises up and calls out, "This is not OK! This is not how it is meant to be." Looking around at the many human rights crises and the climate crisis, there are many legitimate reasons for each of us to be angry.

In the wake of the ongoing rise in anti-Asian hate crimes across North America, I have been very angry, and my community has been very angry. In one year, anti-Asian hate crimes rose over 700 percent in my city alone. This was shocking for many, but I had seen the racism bubbling beneath the surface for some time now. I had heard the snide comments that blamed Asian immigrants for the housing crisis and Asian drivers for the congestion on the roads. I felt misdirected anger and heard politicians blaming Asian communities for spreading a deadly virus in a long-standing pandemic. But even before all that, I spent ten years working in anti–human trafficking efforts and sexual violence prevention and saw all the deadly ways Asian women and femmes are fetishized and exploited. Anti-Asian violence isn't new. And the dangerous part is that when someone is stereotyped, fetishized, and dehumanized, it is significantly easier to violate and kill them. If we do not see the humanity in one another and ourselves, we will not find our way back to one another. And our emotions are a cornerstone of our humanity.

When we honor our emotions, we can release pent-up energy and find healing to the trauma our bodies are seeking to let go of. This is how we begin to befriend our anger. Recognizing that this is happening is the first step. Feeling our emotions allows us to walk a new path, giving space for a brave relationship with our emotions that makes way for healing.

Reflection

* What is your default method of expressing emotions?
* Were you ever dismissed, judged, or shamed for your emotions?
* What message is your body communicating through the expression of your emotions?

Invitation: Embodied Movement Meditation

Through my work as a somatic practitioner and my own personal journey, I've learned that we cannot find true transformation by thinking or talking ourselves to change; it must be felt and embodied physically and, ideally, witnessed and held in community with others who see us and embrace us fully. In March 2020, I started offering something I've come to call Embodied Movement Meditation. At the height of a global pandemic, we would light candles in our bedrooms and show up on Zoom together, separated in our homes but close in spirit. With cameras on or off, we would turn on music and shake the emotions and anxious energy out of our bodies through dance, stretching, tears, screams, tapping, stomping, jumping, and gyrating however our bodies led us.

Powerful moments of transformation happened every single time that we came together. It started small, as a tiny whisper in the core of our hearts and grew into a wild, untamed, unleashed enactment of all the powerful emotions we had been holding inside. Something profound happens when we lower our defenses and release all the emotions we've tucked so tightly inside. Oh, friends, it brings tears to my eyes to think of how holy and sacred those nights of Embodied Movement Meditation are. Throughout the entire pandemic and still today, we are coming together in community to return to right relationship with our bodies and each other. We are unlearning all the lies of shame by relearning all the ways our bodies are wise and safe allies for us. It is something of heaven touching earth when we come together in this way: alive in our bodies to freely feel the full spectrum of human emotions while being held and seen by others.

I hope you experience this goodness in your own body as well. Gather a group together for your own night of Embodied Movement Meditation! It might have started with me, but it is meant to be shared with all who long for a space to be fully their own and share in deep, embodied connection with others. Or join one of the Embodied Movement Meditation nights that I lead. I would love to have you and see your face in the little Zoom square on my computer too!

HOW TO HOST YOUR OWN EMBODIED MOVEMENT MEDITATION EXPERIENCE

* Begin by gathering people you feel safe in your body to be with. These can be trusted friends, family members, or people who are about to become trusted friends.
* Create clear community agreements for your time together. This can include guidelines like:
  o Everyone who attends this experience agrees to keep the participant list confidential and the experiences that unfold during this time confidential.
  o We agree to come to this place with curiosity and not judgment, for both ourselves and others.
  o There will be no disagreeing with others when they share their stories. We understand that no one else knows what it feels like to live in our bodies.
  o We agree to not contact the other participants in this group without invitation or consent.
* Whenever possible, open with an acknowledgment of the Indigenous people of the land you are on; this is a respectful way to be in right relationship with the earth as you begin. (I will discuss this more in later chapters.)

* Begin with a time of breath work, poetry, or guided meditation to help ground you in the present moment. The invitations at the end of each chapter of this book could work well for this purpose.

* Give an opportunity to set your intentions for the experience. If you have come together for a specific purpose or to release a predetermined emotion, now is the time to bring mindfulness to this chosen topic.

* Slowly begin to incorporate movement. Remind each participant to notice what is happening in their bodies as they give safe space for these emotions to release. We listen with our whole personhood to the ways our body seeks to speak to us when we let go.

* Go only where your body is leading. This is not the time for performance or choreography. Don't focus on how it looks; focus on how it feels.

* Take breaks for water and breath. If at any point you feel discomfort or pain, listen to what your body is telling you. There is no need to go at anyone else's pace than your own.

* After about thirty minutes of Embodied Movement Meditation (if you are using music, you might consider approximately fifteen minutes of slow songs and fifteen minutes of active songs), return your breathing to a normal state with a song or two of stretching and slower meditation.

* Finish with a sharing circle if it feels safe enough. Everyone has an opportunity to share as they are fully heard and embraced by the community. You can choose to split this time up any way you'd like. Here are two explorations for your sharing:
  o What did you come here to release?
  o What did you learn here that you will take with you?

* Thank each participant for their presence in the community and send one another on your future journeys.
* Close by reminding each person to transition slowly from
  this space back to "normal" life. Hydrate and nourish your
  body. Be kind and gentle with yourself as you go.

Chapter 4

Healing Trauma

It's not all in your head; trauma lives in your body. Understanding how our trauma shows up in our bodies and impacts our relationships with one another is the key to healing our relationships—not only with just our bodies but with each other as well.

To reclaim our bodies and strike a revolution against body-based oppression, we need to uncover the barriers standing in the way of our embodiment. We need to get curious about the story our body is holding onto. Like many of the clients that I work with, I didn't at first think that I held trauma in my body. The greatest question I had when I started walking the path of my own healing journey and reclaiming embodiment was "Why am I disembodied in the first place?" I never witnessed or experienced anything dramatically traumatic: no car accidents, near-death experiences, school shootings, or armed robberies. I came from a "good family" in a close-knit small town.

But as I began to look closer at the story of my life, I realized that the very world I exist in is one of trauma. I was raised in a church that taught a theology that distanced me from my body. I live in a colonized society where patriarchy, white supremacy, capitalism, and compulsory heteronormativity was the status quo. I may have not experienced one dramatic episode of traumatic chaos, but rather I received a slow compounding of traumatic messages that caused me to separate myself from myself in order to survive. These messages came from the church, my family, my friends, and the culture all around me. Ingesting body hostility every day was poisoning me. Living in a patriarchal society, which taught me I had less worth than a man, was poisoning me. Being raised to submit to men, no matter the personal cost, was poisoning me. Constantly being told that my body and my sexuality was a temptation that could lead others—and myself—to hell was poisoning me. Denial of my queerness and erasure of my Asian heritage was poisoning me. Pushing my body's productivity and ignoring my own natural rhythms for the sake of capitalism was poisoning me. Making myself small, to be perceived as less of a "difficult woman" was poisoning me. In effect, my body was crying out under the suppression of my full self, and the trauma that caused me to disassociate from my authenticity to the point that I could not carry on any longer.

Unwinding these messages was the start of healing and is now the work I do alongside my clients every single day. You see, my situation was not unique. If we have lived under the hostile body systems of patriarchy, colonization, and white supremacy, *we all carry trauma.* Regardless of your personal story, we all have healing to do and if we do not talk about our pain, our bodies will.

How Trauma Lives in Our Bodies

Trauma occurs in our bodies when something happens to us that shifts our inner world in a negative way, causing us to feel trapped, neglected, alone, worthless, or disempowered. Until recently, trauma has been deeply misunderstood by mainstream culture and even the medical community. Sometimes trauma can look like a big singular event, such as fighting in a war, becoming a refugee, having someone close to you pass away violently, or witnessing a car accident. Anyone would point to these experiences and agree that they are deeply traumatic. However, trauma does not have to come from a singular event. It can also be a subtle erosion of safety over time, through consistent neglect or lack of emotional attachment from caregivers, experiencing an unsafe intimate relationship with a partner, going through a divorce, being in isolation, or not having our emotional needs met.

If we grew up in a home with inconsistent or emotionally absent parents, we would try to understand by finding meaning in that experience, perhaps blaming ourselves for their lack of secure attachment in our lives or believing there must be something wrong or broken within us that makes us unlovable. Or perhaps we grew up in a religion that regularly reminded us that we are sinful, desperately wicked people, that our very bodies are bad, and that who we loved was a sin; it doesn't take long for the body to internalize the message that if we are inherently bad in our bodies, then we must disembody ourselves from our very flesh to remain "good," "pure," and "acceptable." It is through the work of healing and coming back into right relationship with our bodies that we can rediscover our true selves again.

Living in a community adds even more complexity. For all intents and purposes, humans are still just pack animals. We live in herds and depend on one another for survival. We like to think we have evolved beyond that, with our modern technologies, well documented research, and innovative advances as a society. But we are still just living in primal, animal bodies. Our survival has always been interdependent on one another, and being isolated from the pack meant the threat of death. This is one of the reasons so many people remain in unhealthy or unsafe friendships, families, marriages, workplaces, or religious communities, even if they are traumatic: if we walk away, we fear rejection, isolation, abandonment, and even death.

Any of these experiences is deeply traumatic, even if others in our lives don't always recognize as them as such. This is because, as Dr. Gabor Maté says, trauma is not what happened to you; it is what happened within you because of what happened to you. It is both an external event (like something that happened relationally between you and another person or something that happened around you, such as witnessing or enduring a violent act) and an internal event (something that happens within you, neurobiologically, as you seek to make sense of an experience you find yourself in). Our bodies are always at work for our survival: remembering, assessing danger, and trying to keep us safe.

The Body Is a Truth Teller

As Bessel van der Kolk explains in *The Body Keeps the Score*, our body never forgets. Our body never lies. I witness the body as a truth teller every day in my work. The body can carry a lot of trauma, pain, and personal burdens. But at some point, the truth of the experience will spill out—as a "break down," serious illness, or a radical decision to change.

A client of mine, Mary, desired radical change for herself and sought me out to walk alongside her though it. As a child, she had been molested by a family member. In our sessions, she began to recall deeply repressed memories that her mind had hidden from her but that her body still remembered. Her body replayed flashes of light coming through an open door when she closed her eyes and imagined the encounter. She had always held a gut intuition and memory of the emotions she felt as a young, scared girl. As we stepped closer to revisiting the moment of abuse through somatic inquiry, she had a shock of pain shoot up her arm and into her shoulder, and she revealed that ever since she was a child, she had endured pain on that side of her body, causing her shoulder and neck to ache for the past twenty-five years. Even as a registered massage therapist, she hadn't been able to get to the source of her pain until our session together. Knowing the way our bodies hold on to trauma and muscle memory, we were able to pinpoint that this pain she had felt in her shoulder was a result of being pushed down and pinned into the bed as a young child. Her body remembered what had happened to her, even if her mind had blocked it out. Her body was a truth teller. Even though every effort of her mind tried to make her forget the pain, her body knew the truth and was demanding accountability and justice for the little girl she once was.

For almost a year, through weekly sessions on Zoom, we spent one hour at a time doing the work to heal. We talked through painful memories and sifted through all the details of her childhood that might have been overlooked by other people but that held deep meaning in her story as a young girl. We cried together and screamed together. We punched pillows and rage danced to metal music. I witnessed the unleashing of her anger as she ripped up pages of a book that a family member who hurt her had given her. With the somatic action of ripping each page, she let go of the power those words held over her and the expectations they had of who they wanted her to be. I sat with her and listened as she shared visions from her ancestors that detailed the injustices they lived through, their dreams for her, and all the intergenerational trauma she was breaking with her courageous act of healing. Eventually she came back into her body, no longer feeling numb and no longer disassociating from her most authentic, embodied self. Today, she is not the same woman as when I first met her. I notice a different freedom in the way she holds her body and claims her space in her life. She stands with more confidence now. The physical pain she held in her shoulder has been released, taking her painful memories and emotional pain with it. She knows who she is and where she is going. She is healing and rising in power for all the women in her lineage who could not do it before. She is setting herself free for the little girl who wanted rescue as a child, and she is finding her own safe haven within her body, something that cannot be taken away.

Mary's story is a powerful testimony of what is possible when we are willing to sit with our pain and learn to trust what our bodies speak to us. Our bodies can hold trauma, yes, but our bodies are also a powerful revolution when we come back into right relationship with them. Embodiment brings back into wholeness what has been severed by trauma. Getting curious about the stories and memories that live on in our bodies is the beginning of healing.

Common Body Responses to Trauma

Once we are cognizant of how our bodies hold trauma, we can begin to unravel it. In an effort to protect us, our nervous system assesses every environment we are in, all day long, to determine which threats are endangering our safety and what we should do about them. When we feel overpowered or out of control, our nervous system sends us into fight, flight, freeze, or fawn to save us from the threat. If we don't heal our nervous system after it is activated from an attack or threat of a potential attack, we can remain in a hypervigilant state that is always on the defensive or feeling threatened at any given moment. The strategy our bodies use to help us defuse the danger depends on what is causing the threat and what has worked for our survival in the past.

Fight

When in the fight response, the body is prepared to fight off any attack, countering the threat of danger by looking more threatening. The goal is to be bigger and scarier than the threat so that the threat backs down. Some might call this "going on the offensive." A person in the fight response can have a temper or aggression that is explosive and unpredictable. Often, we appear to switch on a dime, because as soon as we move out of the window of tolerance and our nervous system is activated, we are ready to spring into action. People in the fight response regularly use the tactics of mocking, taunting, insulting, and shaming. People whose nervous system regularly defaults to the fight response have a "my way or the highway" approach to conflict, needing to have the final say and unwilling to see other perspectives. We are easily reactive the more that the fight response becomes our body's default mechanism, and the more we use the fight response with success, the more frequently we will default to it.

Many of us who are stuck in the fight response were belittled, abused, emotionally neglected, or mocked in the past, and our core motivation is to never feel that way again. We lash out in aggression or begin to bully others. Often we are not conscious of the fact that our pain has caused us to harm others; after the threat has passed, we often feel shame for lashing out aggressively, but we justify our actions with the belief that everyone around us is the villain and we were simply protecting ourselves.

Healing a nervous system that is stuck in the trauma response of fight looks like learning to feel our anger and getting curious about why we are angry in the first place. Anger is a secondary emotion that shields the core emotion we are feeling, such as sadness, abandonment, fear, neglect, or pain. As we explored in the previous chapter, anger shows us that something is wrong. Learning to sit with the discomfort of anger can reveal to us what our body is actually angry about rather than instantly bypassing the reflection and engaging in the knee-jerk response to trauma. When we learn to reflect and pause, we give our nervous system the opportunity to write a new story and reestablish safety so we can begin a new pathway that is less reactionary and aggressive.

Another helpful strategy to healing a body stuck in fight response is the use of somatic experiencing. Developed by Peter A. Levine, PhD, the concept of somatic experiences helps us embody our anger and pain. By engaging in a safe, high-intensity exercise to move through the intense emotions, we allow the cycle to complete in our bodies without lashing out at another person. This can look like shaking, running, boxing with a punching bag, ax throwing, chopping wood, or listening to angsty rage music while flailing around wildly in the privacy of our bedroom.

Befriending our anger is a powerful tool that allows us to sit with the feelings of injustice that arise and get to the root cause rather than misdirecting and perpetuating the harm. It also allows us the opportunity to look at ourselves and others with more curiosity and compassion because we have removed ourselves from "seeing red" and moved into a space of widening the conversation to allow for more nuance and perspective.

Flight

A body in the flight response can look like someone who is constantly in a hurry. We are chronically rushing and keeping ourselves busy so that we avoid the external threat or the discomfort of feeling emotions in our body. When we are stuck in flight mode, we likely feel very uncomfortable with stillness and often like to multitask by always keeping busy. We avoid confrontational conversations because they feel dangerous. People who default to the flight response have a history of ending relationships abruptly or can have a fear of commitment. We feel trapped easily and feel safest when we can leave at any moment. People who regularly find themselves in flight mode are often perceived as highly productive overachievers, and yet their bodies often speak to them through panic attacks, anxiety, irritable bowel syndrome, and other digestive issues.

The flight trauma response often develops in childhood as a coping mechanism when our environment is unstable or unpredictable, leading to dissociation and disembodiment as survival strategies. We learn to be hypervigilant and are ready to leave the environment at any potential threat of danger. In our society driven by capitalism, the flight response is easy to mask by being a workaholic and is often even praised and rewarded. Healing a nervous system that is stuck in the flight response looks like learning to sit in stillness, even when it feels uncomfortable at first. People who learned to survive by leaving unsafe situations will also try to leave their bodies to avoid feeling the discomfort of their emotions. Rewriting this pathway involves the use of somatic skill-building to expand the window of tolerance by spending more time sitting with the discomfort. This allows our body to adjust as the nervous system heals and our comfort zone grows.

Freeze

A body stuck in freeze is like an animal that has attempted to play dead to avoid an attack from a predator. After all, we still live in our animal bodies no matter how progressive and technologically advanced we think we are as a species. When we don't think we can fight off any potential attack and we are unable to physically leave our environments, we often disassociate from our bodies, leaving that part of our connection to our full selves behind. When we are stuck in freeze, we learn to hide our authenticity from the world, because the entire world feels unsafe to us. A person stuck in freeze can feel numb, lost, overwhelmed, or convinced that life is pointless. We have little or no desire to connect with others, and over time, our relationships can begin to fade away. Our pain feels so great that we completely shut down and hide, which often manifests as procras-tination and difficulty in making even small decisions. Feeling any emotion is terrifying because we have locked our emotions away for so long that we are afraid we will be drowned by a tsunami of pain if we open ourselves up again.

A common coping strategy for someone whose body is stuck in freeze can look like endless social media scrolling or TV binging as we seek escape and disassociate from the reality of our life. This survival strategy is often misdiagnosed as depression and rarely seen as the nervous system state that it is.

Small amounts of breath work, stretching, and daily movement can be helpful for a body in freeze to come back into the present moment. Relearn how to notice what sensations and emotions arise in the body and begin to view them with curiosity and compassion rather than judgment. Poise yourself to ask: *What is my body trying to tell me at this moment?* And remember that the pain cannot be more than you, because it is you; you cannot be overpowered by some-thing from inside. Seek the support of someone who is trained in somatics and whose work is trauma-informed to sit with you through this process so that you don't feel afraid for what may arise when you return to the body.

Fawn

The fourth trauma response, uncovered by psychotherapist Pete Walker, is the fawn response. A body trapped in the fawn trauma response has learned to dismiss our own needs to focus on the needs of others to defuse the threat of danger. Many religious trauma survivors, as well as domestic violence survivors and sexual assault survivors, have adapted their nervous system to live in the fawn response. This survival strategy often develops when we feel we must earn love from an emotionally distant parent or partner or when we fear an unpredictable, explosive environment and are trying to calm the aggressor down. This often looks like people-pleasing, talking your way out of situations, or letting others make the decisions. When we fawn, we are often going along with another person's beliefs, values, or desires instead of acknowledging our own beliefs, values, or desires from an authentic, embodied place within. Over time, we can begin to lose sight of what is authentically ours and what we have absorbed from someone else. People who default to the fawn response regularly avoid situations of conflict, fear saying no, and are overly polite or agreeable. This is a very common survival strategy and one of the reasons many people who live in a situation of domestic violence fear leaving and choose instead to endure the abuse.

People whose nervous systems have adapted to the fawn trauma response are often viewed as highly empathetic because our bodies have learned to detect any changes in the moods of others and then quickly work to subdue any potential threat of aggression. People stuck in fawn also often struggle with asserting our own embodied boundaries and feel guilty or afraid when we say no because we fear physical or social backlash. Over time this constant swallowing down and silencing of our own needs and voice leads to self-betrayal, feelings of worthlessness, or physical and emotional exhaustion because we are taking on the emotional labor for everyone else without honoring and listening to our own needs.

Healing a nervous system trapped in fawn looks like learning to establish and respect your own embodied boundaries. This begins by taking the time to evaluate what is important to you and where your personal values truly live. I often walk my clients through a process that I call Embodied Questioning for Truth, a practice that we will go into more detail on in chapter 8. It can be a powerful resource for us to reframe our experiences and reveal limiting beliefs we've held on to. Healing a body stuck in fawn also can look like letting someone know how they made you feel when a line has been crossed in that relationship, your feelings have been hurt, or you have felt unseen.

It is important to note throughout this process that none of the trauma responses should be viewed with judgment or condemnation. None of these trauma responses are bad. On the contrary, these responses keep us alive. Acknowledging our body's default methods of survival begins with recognizing patterns that we have used to reestablish safety when we feel danger. It is primal and human. Once we can recognize our conditioning and coping strategies, we can start to notice when our autonomic nervous system has been activated and begin the process of moving from an activated state to feeling safe and secure again. At some point, our body's alarm system will go off again in an effort to protect us, which is good, but we don't have to stay stuck in that response forever.

It's Not All in the Past

All these stories and experiences of both trauma and joy still live inside us. I always say that when we touch the body, we touch every single experience a person has lived through. We might say, "It's all in the past," but is it? Trauma lives on within us, conditioned in our nervous system and living in our muscle memory, until we are safe enough to face it, sit with it, listen to it, look at it, and take ownership of it. It's not mind over matter. Trauma is a visceral response that lives in our bodies, so our traumas influence our mind and our perception of what is true.

Our trauma can create narratives that follow us into future experiences. For example, if the parents of a child were not very present during their childhood, that child could grow up to believe they are unlovable or unworthy of affection. This is the meaning that can be made through the experience of neglect. This limiting belief will likely show up in the child's future adult relationships, because it still lives in his body, even if it happened twenty years ago. If we do not acknowledge the traumatic stories we hold, we will be unable to consciously process it and heal, causing us to continue to be triggered (fight, flight, freeze, or fawn) in the present. Our body *perceives* danger because it remembers something similar that has happened once before, and it is attempting to protect us from feeling pain or being overpowered as we had been in the past. When our primal body has been activated, it moves to protect us in a way that shuts down our logical brain, and it can become very difficult for us to discern whether we are presently in actual danger or if our body perceives danger due to a trauma response.

Collective Trauma

What if the trauma we must heal from is not only written into our story but woven throughout our collective history? Look anywhere in our world and you will find fragmented, disembodied people trapped in trauma. The social structures that we have created and currently live in are deeply traumatic to authentic, embodied human flourishing. Patriarchy, colonization, and white supremacy are all cornerstones of a capitalist society that prioritizes power and production over people and peace. Gabor Maté explains, "What we call 'civilization' demands the denial of human needs."

The dehumanization that we experience through the systems of our society can look like overworked schedules, eating disorders, high levels of anxiety and depression, narcissism, self-objectification, toxic masculinity, hiding your sexuality, numbness to sensation, dis-association of the body, overthinking, self-harm, feelings of worth-lessness, self-sabotage or self-destructive behavior, panic attacks, and suicidal ideation. All of these come because of trauma from a world that tells us we cannot be who we are and that it is not safe for us, that we will be rejected and abandoned, mocked, or ridiculed if we do not conform. And this is how complex trauma begins to form. We don't want to feel the pain of suffering, so we create a new pattern of behavior to protect ourselves, like a shield or scar tissue over the wounded part of our hearts. This is how we survive.

Our trauma not only impacts the relationship we have within ourselves and with others; it also has very real impacts on our mental and physical health as well. Research into adverse childhood experi-ences, with the first study having been conducted by Dr. Vincent Felitii and Dr. Robert Anda at the Department of Preventive Medi-cine at Kaiser Permanente, San Diego, reveals that our emotional experiences as children deeply affect our physical and mental health, ultimately shaping who we become individually and as a society. Everything from anxiety and depression to chronic health condi-tions, heart disease, cancer, substance use, relationship patterns, and more can all be traced back to exposure to abuse, household dys-function, or societal trauma as children.

When Collective Trauma Shapes Culture

Sometimes the trauma we experience as an individual is shared by many others in our community who have lived through similar traumatic experiences. We already talked about how this impacts our bodies on a personal level. But collective experiences such as racism, sexism, homophobia, transphobia, fatphobia, and ableism are all significant realities in the collective trauma that we carry as a society. For example, Asian Americans have been labeled the model minority, which stems primarily from our collective response to the racism we face as immigrants to North America. We are perceived as docile, submissive, book smart, and hard working. Our typically smaller bodies are not perceived as threatening, and we have used this to keep ourselves safe from racism by flying under the radar, keeping our heads down, and assimilating to survive.

Have you ever wondered why many Asian parents push their children to be overachievers? In a xenophobic and white supremacist world, the children of Asian immigrants are often encouraged to become doctors, nurses, and pharmacists because that keeps us in helping professions and out of harm's way. Asian Americans have perfected the fawning trauma response as a survival strategy. Fawning can keep us safe but can also create problems of its own. Erasure and invisibility of Asian Americans has largely left us out of conversations of racism, even as we face violence, fetishization, and microaggressions every day. The experience of being Asian American is complex, and there are a lot of contributing factors at play. While Asian Americans are not a monolith, we come from a vast continent and do not share all the same practices, teachings, or protocols. We do, however, share a similar experience of "othering" here in North America. And this ties us to other people groups in the BIPOC community. We share the trauma of othering, dehumanization, and exclusion at the hands of colonization and white supremacy.

The Impact of Trauma on Our Relationships

Even after the threat has passed, the trauma lives on in our bodies until we heal it. My Ah Ma tells me stories of surviving World War II, cutting her hair short, binding her chest to look less like a girl, and sleeping in the underground cellar at night to avoid being raped by soldiers during the occupation of Singapore. The fear of sexual assault can live on in our bodies for very long periods of time. Even today, many women, femmes, trans, gender-nonconforming, nonbinary, or Two-Spirit people learn how to live with the very real threat of sexual or physical assault every single day. We learn how to survive by sharing tips on self-defense and how to carry our keys at night, watching our drinks, and sending out GPS locations via text on our phones every time we leave the house. Still, the rape statistic for women in North America is one in three, and the #MeToo movement revealed how documented statistics may never accurately portray the full truth of this sexual assault crisis, because many survivors never report the violence they experience and too many victims never live to tell their story. Male victims of sexual assault also rarely speak out against their perpetrators, resulting in their experience often being minimized and largely ignored.

The result of such widespread sexual violence is often a deep-seated mistrust of people and relationships, which can manifest in a variety of coping strategies. We fear that history will repeat itself, and we put walls up against anyone who might be predatory. While these survival strategies are often necessary for us to feel safe, we need to eventually find a space where we feel "safe enough" with trustworthy humans to unpack the trauma our bodies are holding on to so that we can heal and return to right relationship once again.

How We Heal

How do we reimagine a world with trauma so deeply embedded within it that our very systems, structures, and institutions perpetuate the trauma that we are desperately needing to heal from? Trauma doesn't have to be a scar that we wear on our bodies for the rest of our lives. We can heal and rewrite a new story. In these ways, embodiment work brings us face to face with the stories we are reliving so that we can resolve them. We do this by learning to heal our nervous system from these traumatic experiences so that our bodies are able to release their hypervigilant responses. Finding a way to access feelings of goodness and deep connection amid trauma is a powerful way to rewrite our nervous system and find healing.

We need to heal together, in community and in relationship. This is why somatic therapy and trauma-informed embodiment coaches are so important. These trained professionals can hold and support us when we face our trauma, and they can witness and celebrate when we access our healing. Most of us do not want to think about what caused us so much pain, much less spend time leaning into that very pain that we are trying to avoid. It hurts too much. So our brain protects us by cutting us off from the memory. But like a wound that goes untreated, it will begin to fester and poison us if we do not learn to sit with and feel into the hard feelings so that we can process them in our body and let them go.

Keep reading, dear one. I know the weight of this all feels unbearable right now. But allow yourself to sit with the pain and grief you are feeling in your body at this moment. I could write something light and inspirational to close this chapter out with warm feelings of hope and possibility, but that would again be bypassing the very practice of embodiment that you need most right now.

Go slowly and gently with your body as you begin to heal. Celebrate small victories, and remember that healing is not a linear timeline. There is no need to compare your journey of healing to anyone else's. Liberation is waiting on the other side, but we cannot rush the journey. This is the hard, sticky sweet spot of feeling the weight of it all but knowing, deep in our bodies, that at the end of every long night, dawn arises.

Reflection

* What is your body's visceral response when you hear the word *trauma*?
* Which of the four trauma responses do you identify with most as your default coping strategy? Fight? Flight? Freeze? Fawn?
* With gentle curiosity, can you notice a pattern of what triggers you into a trauma response? Hold the discovery of these triggers with tenderness as each trigger comes from a place within ourselves that is yet to be healed.
* Are there ways that you can offer more curiosity in your interactions with others now that you have a deeper understanding of how trauma shows up in your relationships?

Invitation

* Once you have more clarity about what triggers you and where these triggers come from, allow yourself to get curious about the trauma that may be connected to it. Go slowly with yourself and give your body the space to remember the trauma in a nonthreatening way. If you feel your body's protective walls coming up, it is a signal to slow down, pause, or take a step back. When it comes to healing work, we only go where the body gives full consent and at a pace that feels supportive and "safe enough" to move forward.
* You may feel stretched or uncomfortable as you recall painful memories and look at the trauma that your body is still holding. Try to remain present in your body as much as feels safe enough. We must feel in order to heal.

* Support your body with movement, meditation, reflection, journaling, and other forms of supportive self-care as you move through the waves of emotion. Wrap your body with warm blankets, drink soothing tea, hydrate with water, and feed yourself nutrient-dense soups and stews as you process your trauma.

* Remember that it is not uncommon to feel tired and tender as you move out of a survival state and into healing. This is the time to cocoon your body as you tend to the wounded parts of your heart so that you can heal.

* Seek out the support of a somatic practitioner or take a pause, if it ever feels too overwhelming or not safe enough. We go slowly, at the speed of healing, and you can always take a break and come back if needed.

Chapter 5

Politics, Injustice, and the Body

When disembodiment and broken relationships have been built into the social systems of our world, it is not enough to be body-positive to heal our relationships with our bodies; we must dismantle the hierarchies of body-based oppression and reimagine our world.

My first introduction to the ways that oppressive systems seek to commodify and control the body was when I was twelve years old watching a documentary on TV one evening. I listened intently as a young Thai woman of about twenty-five years old told her story to the camera, sharing what it felt like to have her body bought and sold by strangers who rented her body for their own sexual pleasure every night. It was at this moment that comprehensive consent became a core value of mine. I was forever impacted by the hollow tone of her voice when she looked directly into the camera lens and said, "No one cares about me." She had come to believe the dehumanizing lie that she was only worth what someone would pay for her.

For years her story made me acutely aware of the power imbalances that existed at the intersections of race, gender, sexuality, and socioeconomic status. Oppressive systems place our bodies in a hierarchy that is incredibly hard to escape: those who have power and privilege can rent the bodies of those who do not have power and privilege. Often, people who looked like me—Asian women, non-binary femmes, and trans persons—know acutely what it feels like to be hypersexualized, fetishized, and assaulted under the violent, dominating presence of the politically and socially powerful male gaze. As my friend Istredd says, our humanity as Asians is often fetishized and diminished to a category on Pornhub.

Years after I first heard the story of the woman in Thailand, I moved into my current home and community. I got to know my neighbors, and over time, I learned that one of my neighbors had lost a teenage daughter many years ago. She had been lured into human trafficking by a recruiter who posed as her boyfriend. I had known sex slavery existed in far-off places like my own ancestral Southeast Asia, but now the reality of horrific injustice and body-based exploitation confronted me in my own backyard.

Righting the wrongs of this injustice became my singular focus for many years. From working on a team that amended the Canadian criminal code to working with those on the front lines in red-light districts and recovery homes in Asia, I spent over ten years focused on the liberation of those who were trapped beyond their consent in the sex trade. I saw some of the most heartbreaking things that humanity can do to one another, but I also saw the way that resilience flows in our bodies. Much of my work today is still influenced by what I saw and experienced during that time. I saw how deeply trauma is embedded in our world and how the broken relationships we have with our bodies lead to the broken relationships we use to inflict pain and harm onto others.

Disembodiment and disconnection are evident everywhere in the civil systems of our world. Racism started as a structural economic system that was built on the devaluing of Black, brown, and beige bodies for the economic benefit of white bodies in the ruling class. In his book *My Grandmother's Hands*, Resmaa Menakem does a comprehensive breakdown of the history of white body supremacy and how intergenerational trauma from the European Middle Ages followed settlers to the New World and motivated them to utilize the gruesome punishment systems of medieval torture. He shows how they enacted gruesome violence on Indigenous, Black, and Asian people through colonization and how they destroyed precolonial Turtle Island for the formation of North America as we know it today.

This hierarchy-based value system gave land, security, and rights to some people who were fortunate enough to be born into the right kind of body (white, male, cis-het, abled) and stripped power and autonomy from everyone else. It even went as far as creating laws and systems that enforced servitude on those at the bottom of the politically charged body-power hierarchy by enslaving women through childbearing and domestic servitude, Black people through physical bondage and economic slavery, Asians through destitute working conditions, and Indigenous people through land theft and genocide. The hierarchy viewed everything and everyone in terms of their economic benefit to those at the top. This reduced everything on the planet, including people, to a resource.

As capitalism and colonization took over and established systems of hierarchy, we forgot the covenant of reciprocity that had been woven in the fabric of our collective lives. In her book *Braiding Sweetgrass*, Robin Wall Kimmerer shares this covenant wherein "the well-being of one is linked to the well-being of all" as a living embodiment of community. Kimmerer shares stories of the symbiotic relationships that exist within nature and parallel that symbiotic relationships we are meant to have with each other and all living things. Indigenous teachings refer to living beings in the natural world as "nonhuman kin," including everything from fungi and cedar to salmon and sasquatch, emphasizing the familial relationship we hold with all living things, regardless of species or DNA. When capitalism and colonization took control, we broke the relationships that kept us interconnected with each other and the earth. We began to take from the earth without giving back and without ensuring that the natural cycles of the earth had enough time to regenerate so it could sustain life. We narrowed our definition of family to involve only those who share blood with us rather than remembering the kinship we hold with all of humanity as well as the nonhuman kinship with plants and animals. We forgot that we are all dependent on each other and all part of the same living ecosystem. We traded mutual flourishing for the pursuit of the self, and in that, we lost so much of our humanity and who we truly are.

These days capitalism has so robbed our imagination that we cannot conceive of anything else. Our world has assigned everything a value, so we are constantly evaluating our place in the value hierarchy. We question what we do, what we wear, how we speak, and how we walk to secure our belonging to that place on the socioeconomic and political power hierarchy. Through the pressure we feel from others to confirm, the animal body within us still fears being left behind by the pack and does what it must to ensure our survival. This can have devastatingly unjust consequences, including motivating us to seek admittance into the "club" even if it means harming others or sacrificing our true selves. I've witnessed the impacts of assimilation with my own family members, who intentionally distanced themselves from our Asian heritage to successfully assimilate and integrate into North American culture, a practice that is very common among immigrants. We adjust our accents, change our clothing, leave behind our cultural practices, and even take on new names simply to earn a place of belonging in a new country that provides us with more safety if we appear more Anglo-Saxon.

Once we become more embodied, we may find the ways we have compromised our authenticity to gain more safety by fitting in. It's not enough to be body-positive and feel good in our bodies when the systems and structures of the world around us are built on body-based oppression. So we make ourselves smaller, to be more palatable and less threatening to the corporate and political status quo.

For example, children are not born inherently hating our bodies; we eventually learn to through television programs, advertisements, schoolyard bullying, or pressure from caregivers. Those of us who are queer might have never struggled to embrace our authentic queer identity if we didn't live in such a homophobic culture. Or for those of us who live in dark skin or bigger bodies, we might not attempt to lighten our skin or constrain ourselves to a diet if we hadn't been led to believe that white, thin, and able-bodied were the ideal.

Our bodies know when we self-abandon, and they cry out in pain when we attempt to sever ourselves from our true authenticity in order to fit more neatly within the box predetermined by the structural systems of patriarchy, colonization, and white supremacy. Often, this process is invisible to us because we've been socially conditioned to disembodiment. Body-based oppression has been legislated and normalized so seamlessly that we no longer even notice it.

Societal Systems of Dehumanization

Our world functions through various systems that influence the ways that we move through the world and interact with other humans, the earth, and other animals. These systems and structures have evolved and shaped the world throughout each era. But the driving force behind all of it—all the violence, injustice, and body-based oppression—is economics: power and money. Whether it be the child brothels of Thailand, the refugee crisis of Cambodia, the garbage dumps of

Guatemala, or the water contamination of Indigenous reservations on Canadian soil, I have witnessed firsthand what it looks like when we bow our knee to the gods of power and leave the bodies of people and nonhuman kin as collateral damage. When we've been born into these systems, it is difficult for us to reimagine the world beyond them. But if we look closely, we catch glimpses of a world beyond patriarchy, colonization, and white supremacy; in many ways, QTBI-POC (queer, trans, Black, Indigenous, and people of color) have been doing this decolonizing work for a long time. Through the intersections of embodiment and justice, we can identify all the ways that we have been disembodied and dehumanized. We can also reframe our ways of thinking and being to include collective liberation and leadership rather than hierarchical authoritarianism, which legislates body-based oppression for the gain of power and profit.

Disparities in Health Care Systems

My sister, Shadae, is a powerhouse Indigenous matriarch, known far and wide in Indian country. While we share no blood relation to one another, we adopted each other in a ceremony years ago and have walked through every experience of life together ever since. In May 2021, she asked me to speak next to her at an event for Missing and Murdered Indigenous Women and Girls. I spoke about embodied solidarity, the act of walking together for justice. Shadae hosted the event and introduced all the speakers. In between sessions, Shadae shared a story that offered me a glimpse into her reality as an Indigenous woman navigating the systems of body-based oppression.

Shadae leaned in close to the mic: "A cousin of mine said, 'I need to go to the hospital; I have pain. I wonder what shoes I should wear to be treated right?'" Her words hung in the air around me. As a mixed-race, European and Asian American, woman, I had never needed to think about what shoes I should wear to the hospital to be taken seriously by the medical system. While I do face many microaggressions daily, this is one area that being part of the "model minority" and biracial has offered me a privilege that is inaccessible to my sister. Unfortunately, her reality as an Indigenous woman trying to navigate the medical-industrial complex is not uncommon. A study conducted by Brenda L. Gunn, a professor at the University of Manitoba, examined the healthcare system in Canada and revealed the many ways that Indigenous peoples experience significantly lower health outcomes than non-Indigenous people. While lack of awareness of our own racial bias can be found in many medical staff across North America, it is the *system* that I am personally most critical of. Professor Gunn notes the way that Canada's colonial history has created health disparities by "disrupting Indigenous social, educational and knowledge systems and the outlawing of spiritual and medicinal practices undermined the health status of Indigenous people at the same time that non-Indigenous communities were beginning to benefit from those resources once used to sustain Indigenous peoples."

Similar prejudice exists within the medical system of the United States, where Black mothers and birthing people experience a mortality rate two to six times higher than those in white bodies. Some of the racial biases that permeate the medical system may be remnants of gynecology's blatant racist origins. John Marion Sims, an enslaver credited as the father of modern gynecology, pioneered surgical tools and techniques related to female reproductive health. In 1876, he was named president of the American Medical Association, and by 1880, he had founded the American Gynecological Society. However, his achievements for modern reproductive health came at a horrific cost. Operating out of Montgomery, Alabama,

Sims opened a hospital for enslaved people that he rented, bought, or kept on his property. There he performed medical experiments on their bodies without anesthesia, even though anesthesia was available for use at this time. The common belief was that the skin of Black people was thicker than those of white-skinned folks and as such, they did not feel pain. This approach to medicine was uncontroversial in the South at the time and has persisted among some doctors today, even being printed in medical books until very recently. These are just some of the many ways that the world around us is built on structural body-based oppression and power hierarchies that impact socioeconomic status as well as life-and-death circumstances every single day.

Perhaps things would have been different if traditional healers, medicine men, and wise women had been allowed to continue the ancient practices they passed on through the generations. But colonization did not allow this. A concerted effort by the medical system, the political system, and the church ensured that traditional healers and plant medicine keepers were stamped out. In the 1400s, witchcraft was declared the "single greatest threat to Christian European civilisation," and this idea followed European settlers to Turtle Island (North America), resulting in the notorious Salem Witch Trials, among many other horrific witch hunts. Continuing into the 1800s, the structural systems built by medical doctors, political leaders, and church fathers gave way to witch hunts led by the same people who built, policed, and benefited from the systems. Estimates suggest that the leaders of these patriarchal and colonial systems tortured, executed, and maimed thousands to millions of men, women, and nonbinary people for their involvement or suspicion of involvement in practicing plant medicine, spirituality, or bodily autonomy that operated outside of the medical, political, and religious systems' control. This witch hunt campaign furthered a campaign of terror on the bodies of many who lived outside the colonial ruling class. The message was clear: submit to authoritarian power or suffer the consequences.

Body-Based Oppression and the Law

The postslavery era of the Southern United States enacted a similar message through Jim Crow laws. From the end of the Civil War until 1968, Jim Crow laws were enforced in every state that legalized racial segregation. This was true not just for the Black community but also for people of Asian, Hispanic, and Spanish descent. According to a resource from Georgia College, "these segregation practices affected every aspect of daily life, becoming enforced in professional offices, building entrances, schools, hospitals, asylums, jails, cemeteries, residential homes or neighborhoods, buses, rail cars, restrooms, water fountains, cashier windows, and phone booths. Not only were these institutions and objects separated, but it was also often the case that those for the African American community were not as nice or maintained as well as those for the white community."

A white-dominated vigilante community who believed they were entitled to land and power by birth lynched, tortured, and violated Black bodies simply for taking up space. Even looking at a white-bodied person "the wrong way" could result in a death sentence. And while people of color were legally considered equal, Jim Crow laws and the practice of segregation permeated our bias and laid the groundwork for the social, economic, and political systems of today. These are just a few of the many examples of how our current social, economic, and political systems still function on the body-based systems of oppression that they were built on. This is not just Black history in America, or Indigenous history, or Asian-American history; this is white history too, and it is important for us to treat it as such.

Somatic Exercise: Noticing and Sitting with Discomfort

Let's pause here for a moment. Notice what is happening in your body as you read these chapters on body terrorism and the socio-economic and political systems of structural oppression. Racism and misogyny show up in our bodies in a visceral way. It is traumatic to experience these forms of violence firsthand, but it can also be traumatic to witness them happening to someone else—or even to read about them in a book or watch them in a documentary. This is because our bodies know what justice feels like, like how we know what truth feels like when it resonates in the body. When violence occurs from one body to another, the covenant of reciprocity is broken and we feel it deeply within, even when we try to disassociate and numb ourselves from this inner conflict for our own personal gain. Our collective humanity speaks to us through the sensations and reactions in our bodies.

If you live in the body of a historically oppressed identity, your somatic experience might ignite a fight, flight, freeze, or fawn response in your body. If you live in the body of a historically privileged identity, you may also feel threatened or defensive but for a different reason. Regardless of skin color, no one wants to be called racist. In her book *Recovering Racists: Dismantling White Supremacy and Reclaiming Our Humanity*, my friend Idelette McVicker shares that she had been on a quest for years to prove to the world how she was *not* a racist. She shared the journey of what it takes to somatically heal that feeling of defensiveness in her body so that she can embody antiracism in all the areas of her life.

When our guards go up in self-preservation or we perceive that we are being judged, we are more likely to take things personally. This can cause us to miss one another's intentions, often leading to conflict rather than better understanding. If we live in the body of a historically privileged person, we can feel defensive or guarded when conversations of racism, misogyny, or homophobia come up, and I understand this response. It might be labeled white fragility, but from an understanding of somatics and trauma, I would argue that our reactions go deeper in our bodies than that. Our nervous system activation can begin to feel threatened due to a fear that all the body terrorism we have seen others endure will turn on us as retribution or revenge. As a result, our defenses go up. We can end up interpreting conversations on racism, misogyny, and homophobia as personal accusations against us. Or we fight to get critical race theory banned in schools. Or we argue that the extinction of the Anglo-Saxon people group is coming. Sometimes we actively look for ways to dismiss the experiences of people of color because we feel threatened in our bodies.

Having these feelings does not mean we are bad people. It just means we have inner work we need to do. Let me be clear about this: we *all* have unlearning and decolonizing work to do. After generations of institutionalized oppression in North America, racism is embedded in our nervous systems. It is an experience we all share, and we must all heal from. If you live in a white body, you do not have to feel guilty or defensive for it. If you live in a racially marginalized body, you do not have to attach fear or shame to your identity or maintain an intense pressure to succeed. These are all symptoms of racial trauma. Likewise, internalized racism, misogyny, ableism, and homophobia are all very real. Lateral violence between members of historically oppressed people is also real. These structural systems of oppression permeate everything in our world, so it is important for us to recognize the impacts they have on our relationships. It is impossible for us not to absorb at least a little bit of these toxic ideals, even if they do not align with our personal values for human dignity, equality, and justice. This is why we must be antiracist and liberation-focused in the way we interact with ourselves and the world. Your body is good, and you do not need to apologize for it. Instead of shrinking back in shame, we must be in a continuous process of unlearning, decolonizing, and deconstructing societal messages, while also giving ourselves the time to integrate new liberating beliefs and ways of being in our bodies. We must return to relationship, both with each other and ourselves. This is how we undo the effects of patriarchy, colonization, and white supremacy: by releasing the grip they hold on us and making way for a new, liberated, embodied future.

If these feelings are building inside your body, if you notice resistance anywhere, or if you feel triggered by reading this: I invite you to sit with those uncomfortable feelings as they arise. Triggers and resistance show us the places that we can learn. Try to approach these feelings with curiosity and not judgment.

Where do you notice the sensations begin to build in your body?

Do you feel tightness or openness?

Is there tension anywhere?

Do you feel a desire to run or defend yourself?

What does the building sensation feel like? Does it feel heavy? Is your body hot or cold? Does it cause your body to want to react or move in a certain way?

Do you feel numb? Numbness is a sensation too.

I don't have the specific answers for you; the answer lies within your own body. Building our capacity to sit with big feelings allows us to explore the answers our bodies seek to share with us, without shutting down the conversation. As we sit with the discomfort of these new perspectives, we can expand our view to see things that we couldn't see before, which is where we begin learning and healing.

Coming back to our right relationship with our bodies and noticing the ways our somatic sensations show up within us is a powerful embodiment practice that can lead back to right relationship with one another. It can show us where our biases are and help us uncover limiting beliefs that we have absorbed from the structural systems of body-based oppression that exist all around us. Noticing the shifts within our bodies helps our ability to access nuance and complexity rather than reinforcing a binary way of thinking or an "us versus them" mentality. This helps us to see the humanity within one another and restore the covenant of reciprocity that weaves right relationship within us all. Until we learn to do this, we won't achieve racial justice or collective liberation in the way our bodies long for.

Capitalism, Broken Relationships, and the Body

On the shores of Turtle Island, now known by its colonial name of North America, we live under a system of colonial economics that brought capitalism to the people living here and with it created a hierarchy of land ownership, political power, production, and resource control that placed white settler bodies at the top. This was always about power and profit; white supremacy is always about power and profit. For much of North America's history, it was profitable to be racist, sexist, and ableist.

One of the biggest ways that we commodified the body for profit, power, and gain is through the machine of capitalism, in which we are sold body hatred in a bottle. Pressured to fit a certain body type, we may adjust our bodies so that we can wear the latest style without a "muffin top," hide our age by dyeing our gray hairs, or thin out our bodies so our thighs don't touch when we stand in our bathing suits. But every adjustment we make to our bodies sends a message to our core selves that we aren't worthy enough to be loved or accepted as we are. Over time, these adjustments begin to sever ourselves from our bodies until eventually we are so unhappy in the

bodies we live in that we ultimately feel out of touch and out of relationship with them all together.

Beyond capitalism, we must look at all the ways in which colonization impacts our societal standards of beauty by watering down
diversity in favor of a Eurocentric standard of beauty at best and a
fetishization of QTBIPOC beauty at worst. Colorist prejudice has its
roots in slavery and classism, harking back to a time when people in
poverty had no option but to labor under the hot sun; thus, darker
skin was evidence that you were part of the working class, and the
effects have lingered. In Bollywood, Latinx telenovelas, and the
entertainment industry across Asia, fair-skinned celebrities receive
far more fame than dark-skinned actors, singers, and entertainers—a
reflection of our internalized colorism. When I visit my family in Asia,
I still see pharmacy shelves stocked with all kinds of skin-whitening
products that boast "fair, glass-like skin." This mentality is not only
colorist and built on body-based oppression; it also exposes beauty
seekers to hundreds of skin bleaches and toxic chemicals that can
cause life-threatening conditions. Racism sold to us in pretty pack-
ages with the high price tag of self-loathing and chemical poisons.

Many of us also perpetuate cruelty onto our own bodies. I came
of age at the height of the 1990s and 2000s "heroin chic" super-
model era, and I witnessed almost every single one of my peers developing some kind of disordered eating or unhealthy obsession with
fitness. At the Miss World pageant in 2012, one of my closest friends
in the competition found herself on her hotel room floor, needing
critical medical attention because she had gone days without consuming anything other than a morning cup of coffee. And this isn't
a tragedy that I've seen only in pageant competitions; it can happen
anywhere. Far too often we deprive our bodies of proper nutrient-
dense foods in a misguided effort to make ourselves smaller. Plastic
surgery is commonly used to shave off parts of our noses to fit small

standards and shrink our bodies to fit smaller spaces. Many of us don't even care if such things impact our long-term health. At our core, we feel such a deep, compelling need in our bodies to be safe and have been socially conditioned to believe that our safety comes through beauty, so we are willing to trade anything to achieve the security that safety brings.

When Body Positivity Isn't Enough

What we don't often realize is that this current third wave of the body positivity movement originated to speak about marginalized bodies that we didn't see in the mainstream media due to racism, colorism, and fatphobia. Re-ignited by body liberation and fat liberation activists, the body positivity movement challenged unrealistic and exclusionary beauty standards, as well as the misogyny of diet culture. It was a direct clap back to the supermodels of "heroine chic," but to fully understand and honor the importance of this movement, we must recognize the deeper underlying force behind why some bodies were marginalized and underrepresented in the beauty industry's ugly origins.

In her book *Fearing the Black Body: The Racial Origins of Fat Phobia*, Sabrina Strings unpacks how the marginalization of Black femme bodies began over two hundred years ago and was perpetuated through fabricated "evidence" that was presented to view Black bodies as savage and racially inferior. The goal was to uphold systemic hierarchies by invalidating body diversity and replacing our differences with one body ideal. As a result, larger bodies and darker skin colors became synonymous with poverty, illness, and ignorance. It was a politicized system designed for power and profit. If our aim is to reclaim liberation in our bodies and expand access for all bodies, then it isn't enough to simply feel more positive in our bodies; we must dismantle the systems and hierarchies of oppression that dehumanize us in the first place. We need to return to right relationship, because only a relationship built on kinship and the covenant of reciprocity can take us to body liberation, which runs deeper than simply feeling good in our bodies.

The kinship relationship is critical because economics built on body-hate, racial discrimination, and power hierarchies have always been at the root of capitalism. Slavery turned the body into something that can be owned, traded, and discarded by another human being. Human trafficking turns the body into something that can be owned and exploited. Patriarchy turned the body into something that can be controlled, manipulated, and bent to serve the power of another. All these political, power, and profit systems control the body in nefarious ways.

Capitalism works to erode our humanity in an even more insidious way. Through capitalism the body can be harnessed by the forces of economics. We are fed the lie that through capitalism we can pursue life, liberty, and happiness, when in fact it is through capitalism that we sacrifice our bodies before the gods of money and power. Where there is money to be profited off our bodies—through our labor, through our beauty, or through our voice—there will be greed, exploitation, disembodiment, and destruction. We work our days away and numb ourselves from the embodied voice within that cries out in protest to bring our attention back to the symbiotic relationships that we have abandoned with self, each other, earth, and Spirit.

Instead of thriving in embodied reciprocity with one another, capitalism has found the body's powerful influence and harnessed it for profit and power. It has turned bodies into machines of production rather than beings of experience. And social, political, and economic hierarchies have systematically controlled our world as a result. This is because capitalism views all things as resources that can be profited from. As the trees are cut down and the water bottled up, nature is no longer a living force to be experienced but a resource to be harnessed. Community is no longer a living force to be experienced through deep connection but a resource that brands harness through the use of hashtags and social campaigns to build profit. And most personally, the body is no longer a living force for us to experience but a resource to be harnessed for forty hours a week—and often more, as hustle culture pushes us even harder.

Returning to Collective Care

While Western, colonized worldviews applaud "self-made men," many cultures of color prioritize collective care. Contrary to what I see around me in North America today, many Asian cultures do not navigate the world as individuals but rather consider each person as part of the collective. We live at home with our parents far past the age of eighteen and do not attempt to "strike out" on our own. There is no concept of a "self-made" person, because we know every success is community-made, as is every failure. For many years in my adult life, I lived in a multigenerational home with four generations under one roof. This has had its unique, counternormative challenges, but it taught me how to have grace and compassion for others who are different from me, that I'm not always going to be in the right, that I need to take responsibility for my actions, that my actions and words impact others, and that if an adjustment needs to be made for one person, then the whole family adjusts to accommodate. Looking back on this time we all spent together under one roof, I am so grateful that my children have a deeper relationship with their great-grandmother because of all the years we spent so closely connected.

In contrast, patriarchy and colonization separate us from one another. From 1890 to 1960, the family structure in North America shifted because of the rise of industrialism and early capitalism. This fragmentation separated the nuclear family (two parents living in one house with their children) from the extended family of aunts, uncles, grandparents, and cousins from the village community as a whole. This separation proved to be a financial boon for many industries, which were able to capitalize off selling multiple products to multiple homes. For example, when I lived with my nuclear family, we had a vacuum cleaner at each home; when I lived with my multigenerational family, we had one vacuum unit among us and took turns sharing the domestic workload. There was less product waste, more affordability, and more time spent in relationship with one another. I spent more money, did more work, and was more isolated when I lived on my own with my nuclear family; I built more wealth, invested in more relationships, split the workload, and had more time with my loved ones when I lived in a multigenerational home. This is not to say that everyone has to live with family, either blood family or chosen family. But especially with the current housing crisis and climate crisis in North America, perhaps it is time for us to reevaluate if our way of living is helping us, our relationships, and the earth or if we are working ourselves to death for an American ideal of living that causes more stuff to end up in the landfill, destroying our wallets, mental health, and ecosystems—all while liberating the rich and keeping the working class working. Reciprocity can be applied to everything in our world and every relationship we have. It is the answer to shifting from capitalism and halting the climate crisis. Our relationships with each other are mirrors of our relationship with the earth, and how we treat the land is reflected in the ways we treat humans as well. We use and dispose, leaving not only a devastating trail of broken relationships in our wake but a climate crisis that is consuming more than the earth can sustain. We have forgotten our covenant of reciprocity to each other and the land. Everything is connected, and we are connected to one another. When we heal one relationship, it will lead us down the path to healing our relationships with everyone and everything else. Our escape from the grasp of injustice begins with staring down the forces of patriarchy, colonization, and white supremacy that caused the breakdown of relationships in the first place.

When we enter right relationship with the earth and each other, we can shift our thinking, decolonize our minds, and step outside of the patriarchal, capitalist, and white supremacy hierarchy that was built around us and seeks to harness our bodies for further profit and gain. Embodiment is remembering that we are part of nature and do not exist apart from it or to master over it. It is the difference between power *over* and power *with*. When we reconnect to this truth in our bodies, we see how embodiment is reclaiming the life in our bodies apart from the systemic hustle of production, of capitalism, and of socioeconomic hierarchy that builds structures of power out of people, bodies, and lives. It is reimagining what wealth could look like when we are no longer seeking production and resources as a means of climbing the socioeconomic pyramid. It is redistributing wealth in a matriarchal way that brings circular economics and a foundation of equality to our social lives. It is choosing to be present in the moment, alive in your body, awake to your pleasure, and savoring your rest, even if nothing is getting "accomplished" that productivity could measure.

Reflection

* Have you ever experienced violence, prejudice, or other forms of dehumanization based on the way your body looks or functions? How did this experience feel in your body?
* Have you made any adaptations, such as assimilation, code-switching, or hiding your whole self, in order to feel safer in your body?

* Have you ever unconsciously held a bias toward someone else based on the way their body looks or functions? Where do you think you developed this bias?
* In what ways could you celebrate the intersections of who you are as an act of defiance toward any establishment or ideology that benefited from your oppression?

Invitation

When we realize that we don't have to work to earn our rest or that shutting down our emotions in the name of professionalism and politeness actually perpetuates harm against ourselves and others, we can begin the work of unlearning: decolonizing the influence of capitalism in our bodies. This rejection of the socioeconomic hierarchy is something to be experienced in our bodies when we come back into relationship with them.

Try this embodiment exercise: savoring sensuality. Think back to the moment where you experienced the most pleasure and indescribable joy. Was it when you laughed until your belly hurt and your eyes watered? Was it when your tongue savored the juicy goodness of a food that fueled your body, connected you to culture, and brought you into community with others? Hold this memory in your mind and revisit the goodness of that experience. The moments that we experience the most pleasure tend to come from living in the moment, not overthinking the past or anxiousness of the future but living in the gift of the present.

Now ground yourself in the present moment. What does it feel like to slow down and take big breaths into your lungs? To slow down without needing to earn your rest? To put your phone, email alerts, or social media on silent? To realize that you don't have to instantly respond to each message at the expense of your mental and physical health?

This rejection of our hustle-based society is a rejection of the pressures of capitalism and colonization. When we do this, we move ourselves out of the "rat race" and into a more embodied natural rhythm that listens to the needs of our bodies and the ebb and flow of self-care, collective care, and human-centered thriving rather than profit-centered gain. All these pleasures come from moments when we live in our body: out of our heads and into the fullness of who we are in the present.

Chapter 6

No One Left Behind

Disability justice is giving space for our bodies to exist and reimagining the world so that no one is left behind.

I don't speak of it often, but I live with a chronic condition that causes me pain in my body on a daily basis. In my teenage years, I wore a medical device that covered most of my body, causing others to physically pull back from me after embracing me for a hug. I've spent countless hours receiving treatments at medical facilities and physiotherapy clinics, getting X-rays at hospitals, and pursuing various forms of holistic pain management. Yet at the end of the day, my condition is not something that can be fixed. So I've learned to live with the chronic pain and find management strategies that fit my lifestyle with the least amount of hindrance. I've adapted the way I stand, walk, and move to fit in. Still, if you look closely, you can see the impacts of my condition and trace the stories of its presence through the structure of my bones.

While I don't know the outcome, I've been told by doctors that these impacts will become more and more apparent over time, and I may get to a point where I can no longer hide my condition from the eyes of those around me. These days I climb rocks in the desert and dance in the water because I don't know what the future may hold or if one day I'll still be able to. Yet through it all, my body has taught me that slowing down and listening to her needs is not a sign of weakness but an embrace of my full humanity and a powerful resistance to the status quo of hustle. My body has wisdom and goodness, even amid pain and struggle. In fact, it is the pain and struggle that often teaches me the most and has refined my character. This is not to say that there is always a silver lining to our struggles; when we are in the thick of it, the pain is immensely real and powerful. However, for me, changing my relationship to pain has allowed me to alchemize it so that I can see my body as a teacher. This way I can embrace the truth that the only way through is to lean into it, feel it all, and accept the lessons as they come.

If I had given in to the societal narrative of ableism, I might have begun to resent my body for not performing the way I expected it to. And while there are still many days when the chronic pain and fatigue holds me back from doing things I'd like to do, the practice of embodiment has helped me come back into relationship with my body and find a way to embrace presence in its fullness, allowing myself to feel the full spectrum of humanity from goodness to pain. Truthfully there are many days where the pain is too much and I'm forced to slow down. Because of my chronic condition, pain is my teacher, and I've had to learn to stop myself from pushing through because the consequences of pushing myself to do something she is not capable of is not worth the expectation of keeping up appearances. My worth and belonging are not dependent on what I can do or achieve.

We often don't see this full spectrum of human experiences, including disability and chronic illness, partly due to lack of representation and partly due to the ableism that runs rampant in our society.

Our world is not built for it. From the moment someone is born with a chronic condition, neurodiversity, or in an "abnormal" body of any kind, their parents are told to expect a lower quality of life and even a shortened lifespan. It almost feels as though the message we are telling new parents is that the lives of their precious children aren't worth making space for within our systems. And for those who have lived seemingly "normal" lives in the past—by the idealized standard of health, function, and beauty—becoming disabled or receiving an unexpected diagnosis can create a different experience of grief, mourning, and loss within our bodies.

Tragedy and loss are markers of disability and chronic illness within the systems in which we live. I can't help but wonder, How many of these early deaths are preventable? If our system prioritized reciprocity and access and held a shared balance of power, then perhaps we would see everyone able to enjoy the fullness of their lives in both length and quality. But this isn't the widespread reality today; ableism turns the body into something of an inconvenience and pressures us to push aside those who aren't seen as capable of contributing to productivity. As we continue to unpack the power hierarchies of body-based oppression, we will see that capitalism is the driving force behind ableism. We see those who live in bodies outside of the normative definition of "healthy" as being expendable or even a burden on society.

This mentality of "weakness," illness, or disability being seen as a burden goes back thousands of years within Western culture. Ancient Norse folklore speaks of a practice called Ättestupa, in which the elderly, who were no longer seen as useful, were thrown off a cliff. Several locations within the Nordic countries are allegedly the site of these killings or suicides; regardless of whether their notoriety is based on fact or fiction, their presence in our collective mind still influences our behaviors and attitudes regarding a person's usefulness to society. This mindset continued during the establish-ment of colonization, as sick or disabled bodies remained the focus of targeted killings—especially those in Black, brown, and Indigenous bodies. People who were perceived to be "useless" were killed, aban-doned, or left to die because their only worth was seen in how much labor and profit they could produce for their masters. Even before being sold into slavery, those who found themselves chained on the transatlantic slave ships destined for America regularly witnessed the bodies of those who had fallen ill during the voyage being thrown overboard. Upon arrival, sick bodies were violated with wooden plugs to disguise the grotesque mistreatment they had endured onboard. The intergenerational wounds of these targeted killings are still felt today; in many ways, the residue of this mentality persists within our modern framework of the medical-industrial complex, capitalism, and colonization.

This ableist way of thinking seeped not only into our societal and economic interactions but was legislated within the political frame-work as well. In America between 1867 and 1974, a series of city laws known as the "ugly laws" dictated who was allowed to be seen in public and how. These laws targeted people who were poor, dis-abled, chronically ill, or amputated from moving out freely in public, unless on display or being used as a demonstration, such as the "freak shows" from 1840 to 1940. The preamble from one of the first such laws was established in Chicago in 1881 and stated: "No person who is diseased, maimed, mutilated or in any way deformed so as to be an unsightly or disgusting object or improper person to be allowed in or on the public ways or other public places in this city, or shall therein or thereon expose himself to public view."

The dehumanization was palpable and the consequences deadly. This made collective urban spaces inaccessible to people with dis-abilities, and it left them penniless and socially isolated. It was a death sentence in the name of social cleansing. If you didn't have a family who was financially and socially well off enough to support you, you were resigned to the almshouse for a life of forced sterilization and abuse, stripped of all human dignity. There was nowhere safe to go for people who lived in chronically ill, neurodivergent, or disabled bodies.

But it wasn't only the poor, chronically ill, neurodivergent, and disabled who were targeted. Racism and xenophobia also played a role in the establishment and enforcement of these laws. After the San Francisco gold rush, Chinese immigrants and their descendants were unlawfully quarantined in high numbers to prevent the perceived spread of disease. Jacobus tenBroek was a blind disability activist who was born in Alberta, Canada, in 1911 and immigrated to the United States. He eventually became a well-known American disability activist and college professor who argued that the limitations imposed by the "ugly laws" had little to do with actual disability and everything to do with "society's imagined thoughts of disability difficulties and risks." The last "ugly law" to be enacted was in 1974 in Omaha, Nebraska, when a disabled beggar was arrested in public. The ugly laws were finally repealed in 1990, when the Americans with Disabilities Act was passed. This horrific chapter may have closed within our legislative and legal system, but the remnants of such body-based oppression still exist in everything from bias in our medical-industrial complex to the architecture of our inaccessible grocery stores, event spaces, and shopping malls today.

Charities and nonprofits today often view the people they serve as "clients," depending on their needs for their continued funding and operational costs. This creates a power imbalance and hierarchy between caregiver and disabled person, making it far too easy to dehumanize the person receiving care and reduce them to only their disability or illness. Our lack of awareness of our own ableism often does harm to the very people we seek to support. Survival, at best, is what most people can hope for, and it is no small feat to take on the life-or-death challenge of advocating for yourself or your loved one in a medical system that often analyzes which lives are worthy of saving. There is a glaring need for justice and embodiment at every turn. People don't want to be seen as incompetent or treated as less than. No one wants to be treated as a burden, especially when people who live in bodies that have chronic conditions have so much to teach us about what it means to be fully human. Change desperately needs to occur in our systems and mindsets. If we don't root out ableism from our systems and within ourselves, we will not only lose precious lives to preventable early deaths and eugenics; we will also miss out on all the wisdom that the disability community has to share with us.

Even within the embodiment community, I often see a lack of awareness about the ableism we have absorbed from the systems and structures of oppression that exist all around us. In our efforts to celebrate all that our bodies can accomplish and achieve, we can unknowingly exclude those whose lived experience is different from ours. We celebrate how far we can run, the mountains we can climb, the pilgrimages we can walk, and the freedom with which we can dance, but what if our bodies cannot keep up with this level of exertion? What if we are plagued by chronic pain or the function and makeup of our bodies looks different than the able-bodied norm? What if our bodies and brains have learned to adapt due to trauma, and this source of our survival has now become a barrier that isolates us from the rest of the world? Are we still able to achieve embodiment? And what does embodiment look like when we feel like our bodies have betrayed us through chronic illness, daily pain, disability, or neurodiversity? What does embodiment look like for those of us who experience a different baseline of "normal" and "healthy" outside of the terms typically accepted by the wider society?

One of my followers on social media booked a call with me to ask these very questions. They are nonbinary and chronically disabled. The limitations on their body made them unable to engage with embodiment in the ways we typically see, and they wanted to know if there was something more for them. Together we spent some time exploring different ways that they could connect with their body in a meaningful way, without pushing themselves beyond their capabilities. This interaction made me hyperaware of inclusivity, or lack thereof, and how it's communicated through the ways we set out the invitation of embodiment to others. When the only example of embodiment that we see is ecstatic dance, then we are saying that embodiment is only meant for those who have the physical capability of dance and movement. While dance is one of my favorite ways to connect with my body, it is not the only pathway toward a more embodied relationship with all the parts of myself. There is no performative way that you need to show up in order to prove your embodiment. Embodiment exists for you within, and no one else can determine what it looks like. Embodiment is about cultivating a deep relationship with your body as we build the somatic awareness and skills to understand what our body is speaking to us and reclaim more of our humanity. If we are presenting embodiment in a way that is ableist, we are doing it wrong.

I'm grateful for my friends and clients in the disability community who have invited me into a more expansive experience of embodiment that is not dependent on what my body can do but simply allows my body to be. I'm grateful for my friends and clients in the disability community who have invited me to widen the circle and make more room for diversity. I am grateful for my friends and clients in the disability community who have expressed their needs to me and allowed me to do the same with mine so that we can better take care of one another. It's not about knowing better so that we do better; it's about knowing each other more deeply so that we can do better.

For those of us who are able-bodied, it is hard for us to comprehend the challenges that others live with, but when we are in a relationship with people who have a disability or chronic illness then we no longer have to imagine what their lives are like. Having embodied relationships with my friends who have chronic illnesses and disabilities shows me all the ways we can reimagine the world for better inclusion. And it is my love for them that compels me forward to make greater change in the spaces that I live in. This looks like remembering to have wheelchair-friendly spaces when I plan my events, workshops, and community circles. Remembering to add captions into videos for my friends who are deaf and hard of hearing. Remembering to have safe food options available for friends with life-threatening allergies at events and community gatherings.

Making these adaptations shows that my friends with chronic illness and disabilities are more than considered; they belong. Likewise, when I have a partner or friend who takes the time to understand the chronic pain that I live with on a daily basis, then I feel seen, understood, and loved on a deeper level. I feel safe enough to be honest about my challenges and the areas where I am fragile in my body. It is a relief to not have to keep up with the pace of those who don't share the same medical condition as me. This kind of relationship gives us each space to be human. It is a precious gift that we can give one another.

Praying for Healing

Within many spiritual communities, and certainly within my own evangelical upbringing, I've noticed the "othering" of disabled and chronically ill people through a push toward health and healing in the name of faithfulness and moral superiority. We're told that if we only pray hard enough, tithe enough of our finances, and believe deeply enough, we will be healed. With a family that spoke often about our resurrection in heaven with jeweled crowns, individual mansions, and gold-paved roads, I was regularly assured that one day, Jesus would return to earth, scoop up the faithful among us, and transport us into paradise where we would live in new, flawless bodies forever.

While this sounds like an exhilarating promise filled with hope, the underlying message it leaves us with is that our flawed bodies are disposable and not as holy as the ones we will trade them for when we ascend to heaven. This is one of the many ways that ableism has seeped into mainstream evangelical theology, causing harm to the disability community, cheapening the human experience, and seeing us as problems to be fixed. And yet when the scriptures tell of the resurrected Jesus returning to the group of disciples, he does so in a scarred and maimed body. Resurrection did not transform him into a body without flaws. Each wound from the flogging, the nails, the thorns, and the spear was still present on his body, telling the story of suffering and perseverance, of goodness in his human body that still had more to share. He was whole, even with his scars.

One of the things that my pain—both physical and emotional—has taught me is that pain must be witnessed, held, and honored. However, for many of us the go-to response to pain is to push it down and ignore it. My suspicion is that many of us do not even acknowledge the pain we are living in because we have become so good at disassociating ourselves from our bodies that we no longer hear what they are trying to tell us. And if we do hear when our bodies cry out, many of us experience gaslighting by the medical system and must fight in order to be heard.

Holding Space for the Pain

Being embodied in our pain forces us to feel it, and feeling it hurts. If we do feel it, sometimes we dismiss or downplay our own pain and struggles next to someone else's. We decide that their experience is more painful than ours while invalidating and silencing ourselves. In our empathy, it's easy for us to do this. And while it may appear noble, it does not do anyone any favors. Pain is pain, and each of us experiences it differently. There is room for varying human experiences to be validated; one does not have to cancel the other out. Dismissing our pain to lift up someone else's only contributes to our own erasure and feeds into the further establishments of the binary, in which only some are given the opportunity to be seen, heard, and validated but many are not. Remembering, instead, the covenant of reciprocity allows us to widen our experience and take an expansive view of the human spectrum of experiences that invites more diversity and solidarity among us. This is where we heal our broken relationships with one another, and sometimes even bring healing and witness to our pain. If we do not learn this embodied practice of solidarity in diversity, we continue to resist our pain and try to push it aside, forcing it to grow larger as it longs to be acknowledged.

Validating the pains of our bodies and returning to right relationship with our bodies after illness is something that comes up in many of my client sessions. One of my clients likens this experience to looking around and noticing which of her emotions and physical sensations are sitting with her at the table of her life. Is it physical pain that is present and calling out to be listened to? Or is it emotional pain as a byproduct of physical pain, such as feeling left out and isolated due to illness? Is our physical pain caused by emotional pain or the burden of stress on our bodies? Do we want to rest in our suffering and have our pain be acknowledged for what it is, without trying to fix it? Are we feeling jealous of able-bodied folks when we perceive that our bodies have betrayed us? Are we feeling angry at all the ways the world excludes those with disabilities and chronic illness, grief over all that we have missed, or longing for a future that is different from our current reality?

In our modern, colonial, Western context, we have been socially conditioned to avoid pain and big emotions at any cost. None of us, on any level, want to be suffering. And few of us learned the somatic skills to hold space for big emotions and process the pain and trauma. Allowing each physical sensation and emotional response a seat at our table gives space for each pain to be listened to, validated, and honored. Not only can this practice of listening to our bodies provide us with the information that we need to effectively advocate for ourselves with our medical care providers; it also gives us the space to hold all the tender, painful parts of ourselves with compassion— knowing that we are already whole, even in our pain.

My Brave Friend

In the summer of 2019, my dear friend Christina taught me how to be bravely honest about the limitations of our bodies and how to ask for what we need without feeling compelled to apologize for being human. She was a participant in our annual Miss, Mrs., and Miss Teen BC pageant, and as one of the past winners and a volunteer staff member, I was responsible for all her on-stage training to prepare her for showtime. Soft-spoken, kind, and friendly, Christina stands out from the crowd right away. She is a gorgeous woman, a stunning blend of her mixed Chinese Indian heritage.

Unlike mine, her disability is easy to see. This is not because her illness is visible but because, unlike most beauty queens, Christina keeps her head shaved and uses mobility aids like a walker or wheelchair to help her get around. She has been dynamically disabled by myalgic encephalomyelitis, fibromyalgia, and corresponding comorbidities for nearly fifteen years of her thirty-four years. In her own

words, myalgic encephalomyelitis, or ME for short, is unquestion-
ably the most debilitating and energy-limiting chronic illness that
she suffers from. She most likely developed postviral ME following
a viral infection in 2008, but it went undiagnosed for at least five
years—not because it is rare but because the medical community
is highly unknowledgeable about ME, and it is a disease with a history of severe stigmatization, mischaracterization, and gaslighting.
ME is a highly complex disease that negatively impacts multiple systems throughout her body, causing dysfunction of the neurological,
endocrine, immune, and energy metabolism systems. Her body's
mitochondria no longer produce enough energy to function as a
typical human, resulting in profound fatigue, restricted functional
capacity, and postexertional malaise (PEM). During the pageant,
our long hours of self-development workshops and stage rehearsals
are intensive for any able-bodied person, but for Christina, expend-
ing more energy than the little energy that her body produces could
have long-lasting consequences of aggravated symptoms or a body
crash that could last days, weeks, months, or years. And yet she was
determined to participate in the pageant as something of a personal
achievement while sharing her story and raising awareness of ME
with others. And raise awareness she did.

By knowing Christina and developing a friendship with her, I was
given the opportunity to peek into what the reality of what life was
like for her. During periods of severe ME, she lost the ability to do
basic self-care without severe consequences. The simple act of lift-
ing her arms to wash her hair would trigger pain, severe shortness of
breath, and feeling like she was going to black out. All it took was a
shower for her to be bedridden for the rest of the day. She tells me
about how sometimes there were entire months when she was bedridden. She struggled with her sense of dignity when she reached the
point of needing to be showered by someone else. She felt like her

insides were curling up with shame and defeat. She felt subhuman. With her body constantly in flux of ME symptoms, sometimes her body feels fairly decent and then five minutes later she can be curled up in the fetal position on her bed or fighting a sudden paroxysm of symptoms like nausea, vertigo, and full body tremors. With such unpredictability, she often feels imprisoned in a body that is waging a brutal war on itself.

It was my job to make the on-stage portion of the pageant inclusive for Christina, and in return, she taught me more about diversity and disability than anyone else had in my nine years of organizing the training for the Miss BC show. Movement isn't something that her chronically ill body can do freely or without negative health consequences, so the opening dance number of our stage show had to be adapted so that Christina could be part of it. At the halfway mark of the show, our pageant intentionally swaps out the swimwear competition and instead gives each participant the opportunity to showcase their athletic abilities through sportswear. This gives the delegates a chance to show more of their personality while displaying their talents and athletic abilities. It is set to high-energy music, and each competitor has about fifteen seconds to dance, flip, skateboard, breakdance, cartwheel, dribble, or karate chop their way across the stage. Of course, Christina's body was unable to do such physical demonstrations, so after rehearsals on day one of the pageant, she sat off-stage with me and together we came up with an adaptation that gave her the freedom to authentically show up in her body, exactly as she was. On the finale night, when the curtain opened and the energetic music began, Christina took her turn on stage during the athletic portion and was in no hurry to roll her walker into the center of the stage. Under the big lights, she slowly began to do a few simple tai chi stretches as the audience read a sign posted to her walker that said, "Not every disability is visible." The crowd erupted with cheers. Hiding backstage in the curtains, I found my eyes filling with tears as I witnessed a woman doing exactly what she set out to do. That night wasn't about winning, but Christina won the title of Mrs. Vancouver Island.

Leaving No One Behind

In the years that have followed, Christina and I have remained friends, regularly staying in conversation over social media. In 2020, when the world shut down and we all remained indoors as an unknown virus ripped through the entire world, Christina's voice was at the forefront of my mind, reminding me that during a pandemic, community care looked like extra protection for the most vulnerable among us: the elderly, the immunocompromised, and those with underlying health conditions. We needed to ensure that as many of us as possible made it out of this pandemic alive; anything less was cruel and apathetic. The pandemic solidified for me that in many circumstances, being in right relationship is not about the fulfillment of my rights and desires; it is about the responsibility that we each have to one another in order to survive. People are not a burden or inconvenience when we cannot fulfill the typical and expected roles of our ableist, hetero-patriarchal, and capitalist society. We must consider the limitations that people have and ensure that no one is left behind. *We take care of us*—every person.

Only when we all do our part to care for one another can we dismantle the pillars of individualism and entitlement that were erected within us through patriarchy, colonization, and white supremacy. As Christina showed me, this comes through relationships. By knowing one another and humanizing one another, we are able to strip away all the stereotypes and prejudices we may have and return to right relationship with our bodies and each other. This perspective shift can open the door for us to reimagine the way our world is built so that we may restructure it anew with accessibility for everyone and more compassion for the humanity of our bodies in sickness and in health.

Accessible Embodiment

We need to ensure that the language we use to talk about embodiment and the invitations we set up to experience embodiment are made accessible for everyone. As my friend Christina says, "When things are made accessible for those with chronic illness or disabilities, it inevitably makes things accessible for *everyone*." There is so much to be learned from the disability community. Chronically ill and disabled people remind us that people are valuable not for what they contribute but for who they are. We need representation of embodiment for people like Christina, who are often lying depleted in their beds or on their sofas, drained of all energy, constrained by debilitating symptoms and sick. We need to show embodiment practices beyond the idealized, thin, able-bodied representation to show that we can still be embodied even when we are perpetually ill or unable to be mobile. We need to see our communities built on the pillars of inclusivity, accessibility, and equitability, where those who exist in chronically ill and disabled bodies are acknowledged, considered, consulted, and embraced. We need to see mainstream notions of what embodiment is being challenged, expanded, and informed by a greater diversity of voices so that no one is left out.

True embodiment, as Christina shares, is a "concept and practice that is built on the foundational truths that all bodies are good bodies, all bodies have value and are valued, all bodies are sacred, and all bodies are worth coming home to." Unlike so much of the world that isolates, diminishes, and overlooks chronically ill and disabled people, we need to see our communities become places that recognize the inherent worth of every human being, regardless of age, sex, gender identity, race, socioeconomic status, and ability or disability. This is the vision of my dear friend Christina, and an invitation that I am honored to join with her in re-creating the world. When we can do this, we can rebuild how our society functions by architecting a world built on healing justice, rather than disability. This is our invitation to shift from self-care to collective care.

Can we give our bodies the space to be human again? Can we deconstruct the symptoms of body-based oppression and tear down our own internalized ableism? Can we make more room? More room to be wild, weird, messy, tender, and unwaveringly beautiful? Can we live beyond the pressure of time schedules, normality, expectations, and power hierarchies? Our bodies, in their illness and disability, are an invitation waiting for us. What if those who live in bodies of chronic illness, chronic pain, or differing abilities were given a way out of the capitalist cycle that seeks to devour our humanity in exchange for the accumulation of profit? What if we didn't just roll wheelchairs up to the collective table in rooms with elevator access and scent-free environments but actually built a whole new table that everyone had access to and autonomy to embody their needs without permission or adaptation? What if the only rule was the covenant of reciprocity and ensuring that everyone had a place of belonging?

Now that's the kind of world that I want to live in.

Reflection

* What does your body seek to teach you through the experiences of pain, disability, or illness? How do you speak to yourself, about yourself, and to your body when pain, disability, or illness is present?

* Do you harbor resentment or anger toward your body for the way that she/he/they exist in the world? If so, how does your anger and resentment manifest in your life and in your relationship with your body?
* If you were to get one step closer to resentment, what would you find? Is there an underlying pain hiding beneath your resentment?
* Sit with whatever you find and tend to whatever emotional response is waiting there for you. Give yourself space to witness the pain and listen to what she has to share with you. Hold your body and allow her to exist, exactly as she is in this moment. Take as long as you need to release the emotions that have risen to the surface.
* When you are done, cleanse your face with cool water to bring yourself back into the present moment. Hydrate your body and thank her for showing you the places that you still need to heal.

Invitation

This embodiment practice comes from my friend Christina. For a myriad of medical reasons, physical movement may not be possible or even safe for people with chronic illnesses or disabilities to attempt. Countless hours of my life have been spent in the horizontal. The permanent indentation on my side of the mattress is a telltale sign of the weeks or months I have spent predominantly bedridden. There are times when I haven't been able to move because of fatigue, paralyzing pain, or incapacitating symptoms. I have spent more time lying in bed or on the sofa during daylight hours than I have spent in an office working and more time alone than in the company of family, friends, colleagues, or strangers. This existence is not unique to me; it is the lived reality of millions of chronically ill and disabled people.

Though we are trapped in the horizontal, many of our minds are free to wander. When contemplating how embodiment could be made accessible for the chronically ill and disabled, I began to think about how we might add visualization to our arsenal of embodiment practices for those with mobility and energy constraints. Our minds are incredibly powerful tools that we can tap into, and while deploying our imagination may not come easily to everyone, visualization is a muscle that we can exercise and get better at doing with consistent practice and intentional focus. As a caveat, there may be a facet of visualizing that could be challenging for some. It may be an acutely painful reminder of all the things we cannot do in real life, especially if we fall into the trap of ableist-based wishful thinking where we hyperfocus on our bodies being "fixed." Know that the intention here is not to dream about no longer being ill or disabled; it's about immersing ourselves in imagined visuals that allow us to experience our bodies in ways that serve to heal our relationship with ourselves and others. If it is too challenging to set aside those grief-inducing comparisons, it is OK to acknowledge that visualization isn't the right tool for you. As with anything, choose what feels good and in service of your well-being.

The visualizations I am suggesting here are different from daydreaming. In some ways, daydreaming can be a means of distraction or escape from the reality of what is going on in our bodies. While this may serve as a valuable coping mechanism, with embodiment we are not seeking to escape. We are looking for how we can use our body to become a more fully embodied, connected, and healed person. I see visualization as a platform for creativity, self-expression, and exploration without constraints, which can be quite liberating for those existing in bodies with physical limitations. Sometimes we need to get out of ourselves (in a manner of speaking) in order to be able to see into ourselves with greater clarity.

Visualizations can be used to call us into a state of presence, aid with deescalating our sympathetic nervous system in order to make our bodies feel safer, help us create pockets of inner peace, and are accessible to us wherever we are. They can be done while riding the bus, waiting in a doctor's office, lying in bed, soaking in a bath, or curling up in our favorite chair. They can be as simple as visualizing our hands as water runs over them or as elaborate as wandering through a forest, bringing to life the feel of ferns brushing across our legs, the scent of damp earth beneath our bare feet, and the sound of chirping birds in the landscape of our minds. They can be a way to practice acts of self-care that we may otherwise lack the energy or mobility to carry out in real life. What if we visualized our bodies cocooned in warm waters and in our mind's eye watched as our hands gently glided over our skin, lathering it with soap but also a compassionate touch? What might this evoke in us? Could it remind us that we are worthy of care, kindness, and gentleness? Could it strengthen our resolve to invest in more self-care, however we define that for ourselves?

I have had moments when visualizing an older version of myself who wraps her arms around my five-year-old self has brought me to tears, unlocking a surge of tenderness and compassion for myself that I have never experienced before. There are times when picturing myself dancing with glorious abandon, limbs alight with energy, and a look of pure bliss on my face have rekindled an inner fire—a reminder of my sensuality as a woman and strength in my being that are often obscured by fatigue and from being worn out by perpetual illness. When I visualize a warm, yellow light like liquid sunshine slowly spreading through all my organs and limbs, I foster a peaceful sense of connection to my body and am able to see how miraculous parts of it still are. By visualizing doing something that sparks positive emotions such as joy, contentment, gratitude, or serenity and amplifying how good it feels, oxytocin is released. This in turn downregulates the stress response and moves my body into a parasympathetic state where I can feel safe within myself. Using as many senses as possible and incorporating both breath work and a positive inner dialogue will also strengthen the effect of these visualizations.

Create a space of safety and comfort where you won't be disturbed and carve out time to visualize, explore, and surrender to what arises for you when you close your eyes and open your mind. What do you notice? Where does your mind take you? As we enhance our level of body awareness, we make it possible for us to feel centered, balanced, and whole. Through these visualizations we can influence our energy, move ourselves into a space of self-acceptance and healing, recognize the goodness in our body, and cultivate a newfound sense of appreciation for ourselves that we might have lost along the way. My invitation to you is to use your mind to explore what you need, guide you to the realizations and lessons that are just beneath the surface, and find the peace and joy of being you.

Chapter 7

Beyond the Binary

Our gender expression is an embodiment of our unique human experience. It is more vast, more diverse, more open, and more expansive than a binary could ever hold.

Gender is such a funny thing, isn't it? At the time of writing this, I was nine months pregnant with my third baby. Specifically, I wrote this chapter in between contractions, hoping to finish it all before this baby arrived earthside. (Spoiler: our baby was born about four hours after I wrote this line.) This time, we decided to keep the gender of our baby a surprise; partly because we already have two children—one who identifies as masculine and one who identifies as feminine, but also because gender is something that can shift and evolve over time. And that's a beautiful thing. Whether gender comes from anatomy, personality, or energy, we wanted our baby to have the space to discover these things for themselves. Even if it's only for forty weeks, at least this baby will be allowed to just be human and who they are without any preconceived gender expectations. What would life look like if all of us could live out the entirety of our days with such an experience, liberated from the expectations of the gender binary?

As I've learned more about the intersections of gender, identity, embodiment, and justice, I've become aware of all the ways that we navigate the world in our little boxes, all because of the genitalia we are born with and the gender that is assigned to us. When it comes to gender, the pressures to behave in a certain way begin immediately. One walk down the aisles of any children's clothing store and you can immediately see the socially dominant narrative about how we expect boys and girls to behave. Baby boy clothes will be covered with dinosaurs, dump trucks, and puppies. Baby girl clothes will have unicorns, princesses, and florals from head to toe. Boy clothes have words like "tough" written across them, while baby girl clothes say "sweet" and "princess." Each aisle shares a story of how boys are expected to be loud, messy, and tough while girls are anticipated to be soft, sweet, sassy, and, above all: pretty.

I can't help but wonder how these socially ingrained ideals impact our ability to access our embodiment through a gender expression that exists solely within these narrowly defined categories. As I watch my own children grow and develop, I've witnessed them facing social pressure from their peers to abandon things that they would have otherwise enjoyed. I took note of the ways that my boy had his gender expression policed far more often than my daughter. At one point, his favorite color was pink, and he loved to paint his nails—until he started receiving comments about it from both adults and children alike. My daughter, however, is commended for her interest in stereotypical "boy" things. I have never heard a negative comment on how rough-and-tumble she is, even as she races down the path wearing a princess costume and wielding a plastic sword.

Comparing these two strikingly different experiences of expression is wildly fascinating to me. And while I am no voice of authority on the manifestations of gender expression, I do find it interesting that we tend to shame boys who express their embodied femininity and praise girls for embodying their inherent masculinity. Perhaps centuries' worth of patriarchal dominance still lives in our society, our bodies, and our psyche, resulting in mockery for men who express their femininity and viewing such expression as weakness and passivity. In the eyes of many, it is still an insult to be feminine, even today.

It was not always this way. The concept of gender was not present in many places of the world until colonization and the new colonial system of power that was established all around the world by European settlers; with it came the creation of the gender binary. Across Turtle Island, Two-Spirit people were, and still are, deeply revered in their communities. They fulfill important roles of leadership, guidance, and healing shamanic work. The term *Two-Spirit* encompasses more than just an understanding of gender identity; it also deeply reflects complex Indigenous understandings of gender expression, spirituality, sexuality, and relationships. According to the Ojibwe people, the world is not categorized between two genders. Instead, life is either animate or inanimate and encompasses everything within the human and more-than-human world. This gave space for Ojibwe communities to function outside of the gender binary we know today. People could contribute to collective tasks in whatever ways best suited their abilities instead of according to narrowly defined gender roles. Caregiving of young children and maintaining domestic duties could be taken up by anyone, and many Ojibwe warriors were transgender. But notable Two-Spirit leaders from many different nations exist across Turtle Island, not just the Ojibwe people. In many ways, the very existence of Two-Spirit people speaks of a strong, proud resistance, not only against genocide and colonial oppression, but also against every force of disembodiment designed to strip us of our expansive human expression.

Around the world, gender-nonconforming, transgender, gender-fluid, and nonbinary people have a long history of resistance against the status quo. Their presence maintains that masculinity and femininity are assigned to energetic physiology, not anatomy. Through their rejection of the colonial gender binary, we are welcomed into a way of embodying our humanity that is far more expansive than two little boxes could ever contain. In Hawaii and Tahiti, gender-diverse people are known as *mahu*. In Malaysia and Singapore, they are the *mak nyah*. In Korea, they are the *mudang*. In Zulu, they are the *isangoma*. There is also the Langi tribe of northern Uganda, who have a special group of people known as the *mudoko dako*, which could be embodied by today's standards of an intersex person. However, regardless of sexual orientation or attraction, mudoko dako people were understood to be an expression of physiology more than anything. The Mbuti people embrace gender fluidity, live collaboratively without government, and are strictly egalitarian in their societal structure, with no gender asserting dominance over the other.

Again and again, all over the world, we see the ways that other cultures have traditionally rejected colonial ideals of gender roles and the gender binary, doing so through a vibrant embodiment of community collaboration and collective reciprocity. Here the values of power *with*, rather than power *over*, have allowed such societies to function for thousands of years and survive colonization with a more expansive, embodied, and liberating understanding of the human experience, one that allows people to live out the authenticity that comes from within.

Judith Butler, American philosopher and gender theorist, says that gender is largely a performance. We uphold our assigned gender categories out of social pressure from our peers to do so. Young men must affirm their masculinity or else be taunted and mocked by their peers and their parents. Young women must affirm their femininity or else face social isolation. And for those among us who were born to live outside of the gender binary, an award-winning display of this performance can be the difference between life and death, especially here in the colonized world throughout the last hundred years.

When European settlers seized land and power by establishing colonial rule all around the world, they did so by the creation of the body-based systems of hierarchy that still exist today. White men held power at the top, with white women below them and all the bodies of people of color below, with those who were queer or disabled at the very bottom. Anyone who deviated from this power hierarchy was seen as a threat to the system and often suffered horrific violence as a result. During the period of Indian residential schools, missionaries across Turtle Island were often accused of letting their dogs loose on Two-Spirit people.

But it wasn't just Indigenous people who were hunted and killed for their refusal to conform to the newly created gender binary. Queer, nonbinary, and trans people of every ethnic background lived in the same terror every single day. In many cities across North America, people were arrested for dressing in clothes that didn't match their assigned gender. According to scholar William N. Eskridge Jr., anything considered gender inappropriate was "increasingly considered a sickness and public offense." As such, we see many references to the "three-article rule," whereby gender-fluid people had to be wearing at least three articles of clothing that aligned with their assigned gender. Anything fewer than three articles of clothing, such as a pair of pants, jacket, and tie, would be used to justify such arrests against gender-nonconforming people. The infamous Stonewall riot of June 28, 1969, was one of many raids that sought to criminalize LGBTQ+ people at the Stonewall Inn in Greenwich Village, New York City. Historian Christopher Adam Mitchell notes that in these targeted raids, gay and transgender women were often arrested within the bars, while lesbians and trans men were targeted in bars as well as on the streets. Here, in public, police officers weaponized the law to publicly "check their underwear": an excuse for public sexual assault and humiliation on the street. As the police were so openly violent with their harassment of gender-nonconforming people, other members of the public who shared their views often continued similar violent assaults with impunity, not fearing legal repercussions as the laws, police, and cultural norms were on their side.

Even today, we see many anti-LGBTQ+ legislation being written into law. From banning trans kids from participating in gender-affirming team sports to restricting access to gender-affirming healthcare and even going as far as attempting to label gender-affirming parenting as child abuse, state legislators across America have declared war on LGBTQ+ communities, particularly transgender children. While these actions from lawmakers and lobbyists are horrific and heartbreaking at best, I am most appalled every time I hear a politician or advocate insist that their targeted dehumanization and denied access for queer or transgender children is rooted in family values, morality, and traditional Christian ethics. There is nothing traditional or Christ-like about targeting the most vulnerable children of our society to uphold the power imbalances of a body-based system of oppression such as the gender binary.

God and Gender

If only these modern lawmakers and antitrans activists knew that gender fluidity and transformation has been present in church tradition for centuries. Church history subverts the beliefs that are often held by modern-day North American Christianity. Looking back to the thirteenth to sixteenth century, we see pages upon pages of fleshy, vulva-like illustrations painted onto the prayer books. Medieval church artists and scribes use images of a vulva pouring out blood and amniotic fluid in birth to parallel the belief that Jesus offers new life to those who embody his teachings. The artists' rendering of a vulva on the body of Jesus also shows us a peek into the ways that he embraces a gender-fluid, gender-nonconforming or transgender experience by not shying away from both his masculine and his feminine expression. This makes a lot of sense. If God can transcend culture, space, and time, why could God not, through the person of Jesus, the Christ, also transcend gender?

In many instances throughout the Bible, we see God continuing to embrace a gender-nonconforming or gender-fluid expression that defies any politically motivated, bigoted stance of exclusion that we might see today. In the creation story of Genesis 1:2, God manifests the world into existence. Through this poetry and ancient storytelling, we see God creating everything and calling it *good*, because it *is* good. There is the cosmos and the earth but also everything in between. There is the light of day and darkness of night but also twilight and everything in between. There is male and female but also intersex and everything in between. Being transgender, nonbinary, intersex, Two-Spirit, gender-fluid, or gender-nonconforming *is* the everything in between. And God declared it good, so good, so very, very good!

Some theologians even believe that Adam, the first human, was actually androgynous or nonbinary, gender-fluid, or gender-nonconforming. Or maybe Adam was intersex? We may never know the specific label that would be most appropriate to describe a moment that existed before the creation of language, but regardless, Adam was simply a human in which gender was not part of his identity. But why would it be? Adam was only one of a kind until Eve was born out of him. In this way we see Adam exclaim, at first sight of Eve, that she is part of his own body, made of the same things as he is and part of the same whole. Together, they simply are. All of humanity is interconnected, no matter how different and diverse. We are from the same Source.

Likewise, whenever God self-identifies, it is through the words of "I am that I am" (Exodus 3:14). God does not use pronouns or complex words when self-identifying. God simply is. Sometimes God embodies the masculine energy that exists within all of us, and many verses, written by scribes in a predominantly patriarchal period of time, include descriptions of God's masculinity for us to read. Most notable is the verse in the Lord's Prayer (Matthew 6:9–13; Luke 11:24) that identifies God as "our father." However, there are also references in the Bible that similarly describe God as a mother (Isaiah 66:13), as a womb (Isaiah 42:14), and as having breasts to nourish and comfort (Isaiah 49:15). God is referenced as giving birth, as fierce as a mother bear (Hosea 13:5), and as close as a mother hen (Luke 13:34).

When we deconstruct our limiting perceptions of gender norms that have influenced Western culture, we find that there is nothing to fear in stepping away from the colonial gender binary and all of our liberation and embodiment to gain. After all, if God can self-identify in such nonbinary terms as "I am," and if we are made in God's image, then why can't we do the same? If the early church leader, the Apostle Paul, can state that "there is neither Jew nor Greek, slave nor free, male nor female, for you are all one" (Galatians 3:28), then why are we still not able to hold varying beliefs and expressions of humanity without villainizing one another?

The truth is that our human expression is as diverse as Source itself. We are a vibrant, diverse, inclusive display of heaven's beauty on earth. This is an invitation to step outside of the cages created by gender and live in a more holistic, full, expansive, and liberated experience of who we are and who we can be when we leave the colonial, patriarchal shackles behind.

When Embodying Your Full Gender Expression Is an Act of Revolution

Opening ourselves to the possibility of a more expansive experience of our humanity is both exciting and terrifying. Similar to the story of the stranger with great style that I shared in the introduction of this book, expressing ourselves and specifically expressing our gender in a way that defies traditional gender roles can be very threatening to the status quo. Our world is currently built around the binary of gender norms, and when we step outside of that, people often don't have a blueprint of how to respond. I am grateful for gender-nonconforming people who are willing to muster their courage and reimagine what is possible. Two of my friends, Lee and Istredd, are such trailblazers. By simply living an honest expression of their lives, they are challenging gender norms and making more room for all of us to live our more embodied authenticity. But both of them will tell you that this liberation is hard won.

Istredd always felt feminine or like "one of the girls" for as long as they could remember. But being born in the "wrong" body always prevented them from seeing their reflection match up on the outside with how they felt on the inside. Being a trans femme, nonbinary, first-generation immigrant from Formosa Island (also known as Taiwan), Istredd felt the compounding intersectionality that stood as a barrier to their belonging and made them a target for xenophobia. Immigrating to America with their parents at the age of four, Istredd had always thought that America was the land of the free: a safe space to be whatever you dreamed of. And Istredd dreamed of being fully themselves, a divine feminine yet masculine being, a human not defined by gender but seen by the soul that inhabited their body. Unfortunately, this was not the reality that Istredd experienced. In their own words: "America was a land that accepted the tired, the poor, and those needing refuge, *if* you looked like them and believed like them . . . *if* you were white." Because Istredd was different, they were bullied in kindergarten for not speaking English, made fun of for how feminine they were, and mocked for the "smelly food" they brought to school. As a vulnerable child in a new country and at the tender age of five, they found that the only way they could communicate back was through crying.

One day, Istredd's teacher was so frustrated with their crying and lack of ability to speak English that the teacher shamed them in front of the class and told everyone to tell them to "shut up" if they were crying. At an early age, Istredd was taught that their voice didn't matter and their expression was not appropriate.

Growing up as the child of immigrants, Istredd experienced poverty and a lack of resources for mental health. They experienced emotional neglect and emotional abuse from their parents, but Istredd kept quiet and hid these matters in order to not shame their family or cause them to "lose face" and experience dishonor. During high school, Istredd hid what was happening at home and forced themselves to hold back the tears. As they were assigned male at birth, Istredd came to believe that they needed to "grow a pair" and "suck it up." Istredd came to the conclusion that suffering, abuse, and hardship were just part of growing up in America. As a result, Istredd learned to hide who they were.

However, it was also in high school that Istredd heard a story of a God who loved them unconditionally and declared that Istredd was not a mistake but was fearfully and wonderfully made. When they first came out as gay in 2014 and then as trans in 2019, Istredd saw how quickly Christians in the evangelical church demonstrated a love of God that was entirely conditional, entirely based on their compliance with a cisgender, heteronormative, middle-class, and white expression of what it means to be human.

Likewise, my friend Lee experienced bigotry after coming out as a bisexual and nonbinary mother of two children. Lee, who uses she/her pronouns, wrote about her life experiences in an article for a national publication. At first, Lee was elated at the freedom she felt embodying her truth and thunderous support she received when her writing was published. Unfortunately that celebration was short-lived. Lee knew that the article would surprise her husband's parents, but nothing could have prepared her for what they did next with their reaction. At their kitchen table, over a bowl of strawberries, Lee endured their misguided and bigoted assumptions of what it meant for her to be bisexual and nonbinary. It was their attempt at an intervention. They completely dismissed her declaration of being nonbinary.

"You're a woman," her mother-in-law quipped, as her father-in-law added a backhanded comment about how people in the trans community were losers. They accused her of bringing predators around her children, accused her of cheating on her husband with other women, and equated her sexuality with pedophilia. They claimed she had betrayed them by not coming out to them sooner, and they had the audacity to say that they could forgive her only if she sought *help* in the form of conversion therapy. The passive violence that Lee endured by her in-laws dismissed her entire existence and made her the target of their cruelty. "To come out is to rebuke safety," she tells me, revealing a core truth that is carried in the hearts of the LGBTQ2S+ community. And I, too, feel the weight of her words, as I was outed to my parents by a family member who took it upon herself to tell my parents of my bisexuality before I was ready myself.

For many of us in the LGBTQ2S+ community, these stories are not simply ones that we read but ones that we know—deep in our bones. Our bodies hold the memories of being in danger when we diverge from the binary of gender expression or heteronormative expectations. And our relationships with family members who refuse to fully embrace the vast embodiment of who we are, are often complicated and full of heartbreak. Because Lee works in death care as a mortuary professional, she cares for people after they pass from this world into the next. She tells me stories of families who adamantly deadname their trans children at funerals, refusing to acknowledge their transformations, even if they have been living by their chosen names and true identities well into their adult years. Lee understands the haunting reality that for many trans people who find themselves in her care, their bodies are only there because they were rejected by the very family members who refuse to acknowledge them by their true names. She tells me harrowing stories of needless death due to the fundamentalist and narrow worldview that is grotesquely misaligned with the word of God.

Both Lee and Istredd speak to me of the pain they feel when their families and conservative society wrongly perceive their existence to be a danger to society. And yet they continue to embody something that is beyond definition. They bravely show up and defy the gender binary because the world needs more gender-nonconforming representation; more importantly, trans, nonbinary, gender-fluid, and gender-nonconforming youth need more representation. Istredd says that they will no longer hide who they are "because in all these intersections, the embodiment of trans and gender-nonconforming folks are truly divine. While it may require tremendous emotional labor, energy, and resilience to embody our being in a world that rejects us at every intersection, this is our resistance."

The Embodiment of More

Lee often tells me, "When we stop looking for a solution to our gender expression, we stop viewing it as a problem." And I think she is on to something profound. There is nothing wrong with our humanity when it expands beyond two binary categories. "There is fluidity all around us," she tells me, "and it is in the exact way it is meant to be." My body feels at ease when I hear this simple yet insightful truth. We do not need to fear the ways that we embody more. It is a beautiful thing to be more. Let us no longer settle for small portions of shallow living but, regardless of how we identify, may we audaciously embody the fullness of every part of our humanity and the entire spectrum from masculine to feminine, and everything in between. May we call one another to rise up and bravely hold on to the tender whispers in our soul that invite us into a more expansive, more liberated, and more embodied way of being—more ourselves than ever before.

Reflection

* What does gender mean to you? How do you express it? What does your gender feel like in your body?
* How do you express the fullness of your personhood or one aspect of your personhood through your gender?

Invitation

* Explore what it could look like to embody your gender without the societal constructs of the gender binary:
  ○ What does masculinity feel like in your body?
  ○ What does femininity feel like in your body?
  ○ How does it feel to flow between each gendered energy?
  ○ Embodiment exercise: utilize props, tools, clothing, music, and other forms of expression to play with the different energies and dynamics within your person-hood. How does it feel to embody these different parts of yourself?

Chapter 8

Pleasure

Coming into our sexuality is about more than just welcoming back an often misunderstood piece of who we are. It is about cultivating a safe space for exploration and play, for deeper intimacy with all the parts of ourselves, and for reverence for our whole personhood.

I remember when I first awoke to the presence of my sexuality. It had nothing to do with arousal or desire for another person. I simply discovered that I could feel pleasure in my own body, that sexuality and sexual expression was part of my humanity. There was no male gaze that my first sexual awakening was filtered through. My body simply felt the presence of an erotic energy flowing through me. I was becoming aware of my embodiment as a sexual being apart from anything or anyone else; my sexuality was simply a part of me that existed.

Like most children, I was innocent and naive about sex but was naturally curious about bodies, my own and others. Aside from visits to the women's changing room at the local swimming pool, I never saw visuals of human bodies—or naked human bodies, specifically. Any human form without clothing was something I was quickly ushered away from or told hastily to cover my eyes. The unspoken message I received was that bodies were inherently shameful and not to be seen. Even in my preschool years, I could sense from the behaviors of the adults around me that bodies were something that we didn't talk about. I had no concept or understanding of sex or sexuality at this point, but bodies—something I could see, touch, and interact with in my world around me—were clearly something to be feared and avoided. Naturally, this lack of open communication made me even more curious, and like most children around the age of four to six years old, I began to explore my own body with my own hands. It was innocent. My longing to have an understanding of and relationship with my body was clearly present, even at a young age.

One night, when I was approximately six or seven years old, I remember my mother coming into my room to check on us before she went to bed. She lifted my fingers to her nose, made a face of disgust and asked me if I had touched myself. Unaware that I had done anything "wrong," I said yes and was immediately given an explanation into why the vagina was dirty and that I must never ever touch my own body for any reason ever again.

These messages of body shame stuck with me for many years and were only exacerbated by the purity culture movement of the 1990s and 2000s. Like most of my peers in the evangelical church, I was swept up in a subculture of purity rings and abstinence pledges. Completely lacking sex education, we believed that our bodies were physically dirty and inherently sinful. We read books on how to say goodbye to dating, how to win the battle against sexual immorality by bouncing our eyes away from any person we thought was attractive, who could wear a white wedding dress, and how maintaining our purity made us more captivating to our future spouses one day. We sat through sermons that taught us how sex outside of marriage made us chewed-up pieces of gum. Church leaders compared our bodies to long-stemmed red roses, assuring our teenage selves that every time we consensually (or even nonconsensually) engaged in any form of physical or sexual intimacy with another person—from holding hands to penetrative sex—we were giving pieces of ourselves away and would one day be left with nothing but an ugly, bare stick to give our future spouse. Everything revolved around the future prospect of marriage, and if we could just keep our bodies on lockdown until such time as we met "the one" at the altar, we would be perceived by our community as good, pure, faithful, and holy.

Even outside of the church I encountered messages that taught me the body was dirty and impure. One glance down the feminine hygiene aisle at the local pharmacy provided me with the message that my body—and, more specifically, my vulva and vagina—was dirty and required a wide array of cleansing products that were scented with hydrangeas, roses, and lavender to mask the smell of my natural nectar. In modern North America, up to 57 percent of women have used "feminine hygiene" products to clean their vaginas in the last year, even though vaginas are self-cleaning and don't require additional soaps. And more than 50 percent of women report that they are encouraged to do so by their sexual partner, with 77 percent of young women more likely to succumb to this pressure for their partner's benefit. Shame upon shame is sold with a hefty price tag of disembodiment. It should go without saying that introducing such chemicals to a sensitive PH-balanced mucus membrane of our bodies might have some negative or even toxic consequences. These practices strip the vagina of healthy, protective bacteria and lubrication, increasing a woman's risk of getting HIV by almost four times, as well as increasing the risk of bacterial vaginosis and gonorrhea. But many of us don't realize how harmful these products are for our bodies.

Not only do these teachings give us an unhealthy view of sex, bodies, and relationships, but they also biologically and emotionally alter the relationships we have with ourselves. Our bodies respond to the physiological experiences we have, and the impact of absorbing the shame of purity culture and our sex-negative society eventually shows up in our bodies. Through my work as a somatic practitioner and birth doula, I regularly partner with pelvic physiotherapists. On numerous occasions they have told me the connection they see of women and femmes in the church experiencing higher rates of sexual dysfunction. They tell me how the pelvic muscles that stretch from pubic bone to tailbone hold tension when we are stressed or traumatized. These muscles can shift and change due to the trauma that we receive from an environment where sex and bodies were shamed. These are rising trends among those of us who come from a conservative religious background or who came of age within purity culture. Sexual dysfunctions and conditions of chronic pain are widespread. This can look like:

- Vaginismus: an uncontrollable condition in which the body's automatic reaction to some or all forms of vaginal penetration results in involuntary muscle spasms that are painful.
- Vulvadynia and vestibulodynia: conditions in which the vulva or vestibule (entrance to the vagina) are in constant or regular pain such as burning, stinging, or itching without an identifiable cause. It can be exacerbated from prolonged sitting, fitted pants, tampon insertion, and sexual penetration.
- Dyspareunia: painful intercourse that persists before, during, or after penetration. It is historically understood as being influenced by physiological factors that cause physical sensations of pain in the body.
- Hypersensitivity or erectile dysfunction: a common condition in penis owners that is described as painful,

overstimulation when touched, or an inability to maintain an erection due to past experiences of trauma.

- Panic attacks and flashbacks: an experience of intense fear or discomfort with body sensations that includes heart palpitations, sweating, trembling or shaking, feeling of choking, chest pain, nausea, feeling dizzy, derealization or depersonalization (being detached from reality or oneself), fear of losing control, fear of dying, numbness, tingling, chills, or hot flashes.
- Anxiety: excessive worry, restlessness, easily fatigued, difficulty concentrating, muscle tension, and sleep disturbance.
- Depression: persistent feelings of sadness or lack of enjoyment for previously enjoyed activities.
- Autoimmune disease: a physical condition in which the body's natural immune system can't determine the difference between its own cells and foreign cells that are evidence of incoming danger. This is common in purity culture and religious trauma survivors who have been told by theology that their bodies are bad; after a while, our bodies start to turn on themselves.

These symptoms can induce painful sex or inflammation, making it even more difficult to connect with our bodies in a sexual way.

Many survivors of sexual violence, rape, harassment, and sexual assault also experience disembodiment after sexual trauma. Regardless of what happened to us, many of us were taught to build our relationships with our vulvas and vaginas on a foundation of shame.

In an attempt to heal the parts of ourselves that were pushed aside by sexual shame and abuse, many of us look to books, podcasts, and talk therapy. And these are all fantastic resources, many of them easily available to us with low barriers of access. However, after years of working alongside sexual trauma survivors, I have found that we cannot heal trauma if we do not return to integrated relationship with our bodies, establishing healing in our nervous systems and a safe space to be compassionately seen and held. Those of us who have experienced any kind of trauma leave our bodies for good reason. Reclaiming our embodiment means asking our minds to remember why we left our bodies in the first place; but without proper support, this can be very difficult, emotional, and overwhelming work.

As an embodiment coach, I find that the number one reason that people seek me out is to heal the trauma that lives in their bodies. They need a safe space to talk about the things they struggle with and that they have kept hidden, and they need to come back into connection with all the parts of themselves: mind, body, and soul. They need a safe space to build a relationship with the sexual parts of themselves and learn how to do this in an ethical, life-giving way.

Sexual shame and shame around intimacy with our bodies are perhaps some of the most deeply rooted wounds that we carry. Far too many of us feel unloved, unsafe, or repulsed for the very natural sexual desires and eroticism that we hold as human beings. To be human is to be sensual, erotic, and sexual. But since the onset of colonial power, a very strategic and targeted smear campaign has aligned sexuality with moral depravity and chastity with pious purity. This shaming approach to sexuality impacts us on both a collective level as well as an intimate personal level.

How We Heal a Nervous System Impacted by Sexual Trauma

One of the tools that I have developed and regularly use with my clients is called Embodied Questioning for Truth. It's a simple exercise that invites us into our bodies to uncover and release shame. It is effective because within each of our bodies, we still hold limiting beliefs that are either no longer serving us or no longer reflective of the values we want to embody. We hear the sex-negative messages from others or overthink the insecurities we have about our bodies. Embodied Questioning for Truth helps us to identify where those messages are coming from and whether the voice in our head is ours. Embodied Questioning for Truth can be done on your own, with a trusted support person or with the guidance of a somatic practitioner.

You will want to begin by getting into a comfortable position, whatever that looks like for you, and grounding yourself into your feeling body rather than your cognitive brain. Take some deep breaths and notice the way that your body feels as the oxygen circulates all the way through you. You do not have to remain seated for this exercise; allow your body to move however it desires. Feel your body touching the surface below you. Wiggle your toes and move your hands.

The goal is to awaken your somatic awareness and bring attention to all the parts of your body so that you can connect with your embodied self and fully take up your space. When you are ready, begin by asking your body a series of questions, pausing after each one to notice the sensations and emotions that arise within. Notice where there is tightness, tension, pain, resistance, or restriction within you; these are some of the ways your body says no.

Likewise, notice where there is lightness, openness, peace, or the tingle of pleasure and joy; these are some of the ways your body says yes. Notice if colors, visuals, messages, or memories awaken within you after any of the questions; this is another way that your body can speak to you.

We do not come to the body with an agenda but rather seeking to better understand. Be careful not to look at what the body reveals to you with judgment, but rather lean into the sharing of information with curiosity and compassion. The questions you ask can be on the topic of anything you wish to find embodied answers for. But for the purposes of this conversation of reclaiming our sexual selves after trauma, we will be using that foundation as a guide.

Questions to ask your embodied self:

- When was the first time I heard this belief about my body or sexuality?
- Where does this voice come from? Does it come from within me or outside me?
- If the voice is not my own, who spoke it over me? What was my relationship to that person, ideology, or institution?
- How does this idea manifest in my life? Does it make me more of the person I want to be or less of the person I want to be?
- Is this idea serving me?
- Is it true?
- What do I want to do with the information my body has given me?

Slow down and listen to your body's response to each question. Sometimes the answers are subtle, but when we meet with our bodies, we will often find them waiting, eager to show us what we need to see. At this point in the questioning, it is often clear where the voice comes from and whether we want to keep it in our lives or not. Once we have gained deeper insight through communication with our bodies, we can move on to the next step of the process and utilize somatic skills to help our bodies process what we have uncovered and release what we need to let go of.

Through somatic experiences, we step into the language of our bodies and give them the space they need to process big things, release what no longer serves us, and integrate what will nourish us deeper into the people we want to become. Unlike the mind, the body needs to physically move through something to fully understand it. This is the difference between cognitive knowledge and embodied knowledge. Embodied knowledge needs to land in our bodies and have the space to take root within us. I liken this process to the difference between reading about the tropical shorelines of my ancestral homeland of Singapore and walking them with my own two feet; it feels different when my body knows something through experience.

Somatic processing is the same. This is why humans throughout history have created rituals. Rituals and ceremonies allow our bodies the space to move through life's big transitions. In our modern western culture, there is a noticeable absence of such rituals and ceremonies. Aside from yearly birthdays and New Year's Eve celebrations, the most familiar coming-of-age ritual that we hold in Western culture is that of high school graduation. For many of us, this milestone marks a significant shift in our lives, from childhood and youth to adulthood and independence. We look forward to this day for many years and a series of traditional celebrations are usually held to mark the occasion. From senior prom to graduation cruises, family dinners to memorable gifts, graduation parties to the cap and gown ceremony: many families and communities here in the West place heavy importance on the ritual of high school graduation.

But does anything magical happen in the fleeting moments that we cross the stage and move our cap tassel from the left to the right? No. Graduation, as many of us have experienced, is a years-long process of finalizing our formal education and preparing for life

outside of secondary school. It is a transition that culminates in ceremony, but in practice, we get there slowly with every step forward
and personal triumph we make. Supporting our bodies through life
transitions and using somatic skills to guide us is the same in many
ways. When going through a personal season of growth and transition, we don't cross over instantly to the other side. It is often a long
process of personal reflection, perseverance, and movement of our
bodies through the ritual of transition so that we can grow, release
and renew. When we are using somatic skills to release sexual shame
and self-judgment that we carry within us, it is the same.

There are many different ways to incorporate somatic processing into your healing journey, and the process will be unique for all
of us. Please do not compare your own process to the healing journey of others or fall into the trap of believing that there is one way
to access healing. There's not. What works for one person may not
work for you and vice versa. The goal is simply to give yourself the
space to move through the big emotions and unresolved trauma that
may arise when you look into your body. Processing those emotions
might happen through movement, journaling, grieving, screaming, or
speaking all the things that you never had the opportunity to say in
the moment that the trauma first happened.

Reestablishing a Healthy Sexual Ethic

Those of us who were raised in the abstinence-only sex education of
purity culture or who disassociated from our bodies due to an experience of sexual violence often struggle to know where to go after we
heal the trauma in our bodies. It's one thing to recognize the ways
that purity culture or sexual violence impacted us, it's another thing
to step into the process of healing from the trauma—and it's a differ-

ent thing entirely to rebuild a healthy sexual ethic when we are out the other side. But this is where we must go next in our journeys of healing our relationships with our bodies and each other. For without establishing a healthy sexual ethic, we'll be more prone to repeat the cycles of the past rather than forging forward into a brave and embodied future of sexual liberation.

As we venture forward into sexual exploration, it is important to remember that everyone's version of sexual liberation will look different—and that's good! Let us move from the binary thinking of "good versus bad" embedded within purity culture and give more space for curiosity and authentic expression. With embodied boundaries and consent as our compass, we can find a new world of sexual experiences that are trauma-informed, gender-affirming, risk-aware, and pleasure-centric. This is how we engage with our sexuality and sexual experience in right relationship.

For me, the foundation of my sexual ethics is to do no harm and leave people better than I found them. I work as carefully as I can to consistently embody this value across all areas of my life and especially in my sex life. To do this effectively, I need to meet each person in the fullness of their humanity. When I read the scriptures, I have noticed that the guiding principle of biblical sexual ethics can be distilled down to this: any form of sex that strips another person of their humanity is a sin. This is why sexual violence is a sin. It has nothing to do with the specifics of what people are choosing to do in their bedrooms and everything to do with whether we are trampling the sacredness of another human through violence, dismission, cruelty, and harm. It has nothing to do with whether sex is happening outside of marriage or not, because anyone who has survived an abusive marriage can tell you that a wedding ring and a marriage license don't make a relationship safe. A lack of personal ethics and presence of power imbalances exist even in marriages that present as "good" to the outside world looking in.

So how do we establish a healthy sexual ethic in alignment with our values and beliefs? Where is the roadmap forward in a sex-negative culture that withholds comprehensive sex education from us and instead burdens us with shame in our bodies? It all comes down to right relationship with our bodies and each other. When we can compassionately reclaim ourselves as fully human, we are then able to view the beauty and complexity of humanity in one another. For us to engage with one another's sexual bodies in a way that is truly ethical, we need to go within and listen to all the ways our bodies want to share wisdom with us. This is how we determine our own core values and the foundation of our sexual ethics. Unlike in purity culture, where sexual ethics of abstinence were imposed on us, sexual liberation opens the doors for discovery in alignment with our own values and beliefs.

This shift does not mean that sexual liberation or a sex-positive mindset is a boundary-less free-for-all! Quite the opposite; being sex-positive is about connection, freedom of expression, bodily autonomy, accountability between partners, reverence for our whole personhood, practicing consent, rejecting shame, having freedom of choice, being empowered in your own sexual sovereignty, and having comprehensive, accessible education about sex. When you think about your core values, think about the kind of person that you want to be. Think about how you want to feel after a sexual experience ends and how you want the other person to feel as well. It all comes down to how we ethically treat ourselves and others. We cannot control other people's thoughts, feelings, or actions, but we can take responsibility for the way we treat them in every encounter and know that we did our best to treat them with the dignity and respect that they deserve as a fellow human being. This becomes the foundation of our sexual ethics and our core values that we embody as a sexually liberated person.

While it is of deep importance to handle every human we touch with care, it is just as important, if not more important, to extend that same loving tenderness to our own selves. When we know what unconditional love feels like in our bodies, then we are better able to extend the same compassion and care to others as well. Our bodies deserve nothing less than our love, respect, and devotion. This is where the sweet nectar of our life source flows from, and there is nothing more soul-crushing than watching a person betray their own authenticity in order to prioritize the needs and desires of others at the cost of themselves. If you want to experience wild, juicy, orgasmic, healing sex and sexuality, then you must first listen to the embodied boundaries of your own body.

Embodied Boundaries

Embodied boundaries come out of the full body *yes* sensation or the resistant *no* sensation. For me, if it's not a full body, *orgasmic* yes, then it's a no. I am unwilling to go anywhere that my body does not give full consent. This is because my body knows what is good for me, and when I listen to her warnings, I will always make the right choice in each situation. Following the guidance of embodied boundaries is a profoundly intimate embodiment practice. Unlike the conventional definition of boundaries that is filled with "should" expectations, embodied boundaries are deeply attuned to your personal self-care needs so that you can show up as your most authentic self. Embodied boundaries originate from within you and can only be discovered by knowing yourself, communicating internally with your body, and bravely showing up as your full self with the people who have proven themselves to be safe and trustworthy. I can guide you in the direction of your own embodied boundaries, but only you can determine what boundaries you need to enforce at this specific point in your life. It's OK if embodied boundaries feel foreign to you at first; that can happen when our nervous system has been adjusted to feel familiar in chaos. Start by noticing where your body tightens and where your body opens. This is how we can determine which decision is right for us.

Embodied boundaries are essential to healthy, embodied sexual experiences, even if the only person we are having sex with is ourselves. For people who are on the asexual spectrum or who are reclaiming their bodies after purity culture and sexual trauma, masturbation can be a deeply healing practice of reclaiming bodily autonomy and getting to know our own personal desires. Masturbation can also be a safe way to engage in a somatic practice known as pleasure mapping, which invites you to get curious about all the different parts of your body: from your head to your toes, to discover what feels good and pleasurable to you. Through each of these practices it is so important to move forward at the pace of your own body and with your body's full consent.

Yes, asking your own body for consent is important too and not something to be overlooked. For me, this has looked like cupping my genitals and allowing my body to slowly open, melting into the presence of my own touch. This simple act of displaying gentleness and respect to my body is a defiant act to any status quo of commodification, fetishization, and control. It is a restoring of my human dignity and a returning to right relationship with every piece of myself.

Autonomy and fully embodied consent must be the foundation of our core values, our sexual ethics, and all our sexual experiences. For consent to be present in our sexual experiences, it needs to be freely given prior to the experience beginning and be comprehensive and informed as well as inclusive of any risks that could be involved in choosing to move forward into this experience. This means an open discussion of sexually transmitted infection (STI) status, birth control options, awareness of the physical risks that could be involved (i.e., potential repercussions of impact play and other forms of kink and BDSM expression), and disclosure of any other partners that each person may be romantically or sexually attached to at the time of the sexual experience.

By engaging in open dialogue on these important points, we are able to make a fully informed decision and decide if this experience is the right sexual experience for us or not. There is no shortage of great sex available in the world, and in my personal experience, the best sexual encounters are always the ones where consent is present, ongoing, and embodied.

A nonexhaustive list of what practicing ongoing consent can look like:

- Making space for yourself and your lover to get radically honest about needs, desires, and boundaries.
- Openly sharing STI status and other relevant medical information that allows us to engage with one another in a loving and safe way.
- Going at the pace of your body and your lover's body; there is no reason to put on a performance or rush to orgasm.
- Talking through feelings and intentions before beginning the sexual experience. What do you want to experience during your time together? Are there any new things you'd like to explore? Are there toys you want to incorporate? Is there anything in your mind that you'd like to let go of before beginning?

- Communicate any past traumas or triggers that still linger in your body and that you'd like to avoid until you have the resources and capacity to process them.
- Checking in with yourself and your lover throughout the experience to ensure you are both still enthusiastically enjoying the experience.
- Watching your partner's body language to notice any shifts in mood and enthusiasm. Noticing your own body's sensations to catch any shifts in mood or enthusiasm as well.
- Use of a safe word to end the experience abruptly if you become triggered or simply no longer interested in continuing.
- The freedom to debrief openly with your lover after the encounter has ended and share with them what you enjoyed, what you want more of, and what didn't work for you, without fear of repercussion or retribution for what you have to say.

If your partner does communicate a no to you, there are many compassionate ways to support their boundaries and sovereignty in your sexual experiences together. Encourage them to share their nos with you, and don't take their feedback as a personal criticism in any way. Everybody is unique and has different things that they like or don't like. There are many varied factors at play that impact arousal, and getting turned on is just as much a physical experience as it is mental and emotional. It does us no good to project our fears of abandonment or inadequacy onto a partner who is taking the time to communicate a boundary with us. If you are gifted with a lover who is communicating with you in this way, celebrate them and thank them for their honesty! This kind of radical communication can be very hard and vulnerable for many of us, but it opens up the pathway to the kind of sexual experience that we truly desire, unlocking the kind of sex that we not only crave but that also has the ability to heal us somatically and emotionally.

Reclaiming the Erotic Self

How do we determine what kind of sex we want? For many of us, this seemingly simple question can leave us feeling lost, especially if we are burdened by shame, disconnected from our bodies, or still getting to know our bodies through an embodied relationship. I've worked with many clients who struggle to tell the difference between trauma, low libido, and a lack of awareness of their sexual desires. Your sexual expression can feel unsafe in your body when you've faced trauma and sexual violence in the past. But as with all things, you can heal and reclaim all the parts of yourself, including your sexual and erotic self. Understanding and building a relationship with our desires is an essential part of coming back home to our full selves. As we've said already, our sexual selves are an integral and essential part of our human experience, even if we identify somewhere on the asexuality spectrum.

Begin by noticing what lights you up and gets your sexual curiosity stirring. Remember the goal is not to approach ourselves with judgment but rather to move beyond the patriarchal, colonial binary of "good versus bad" and toward listening to the wisdom of our bodies within. Here we can play with all the dynamics of our eroticism, through the foundational core value of consent and bestowing human dignity to each person we engage with. As you move forward, free of shame, you can begin to follow your curiosity to discover new and wonderful things. The possibilities to play with your erotic self and embody all the parts of your humanity are endless; one of the reasons why I find the work of sexual liberation so important! It doesn't matter if the sex you desire is considered "kinky" or "vanilla" by anyone else's standards. The good stuff we are after is deeply connected, safe, trusted, embodied sex where we can express our full selves. Great sex is about unlearning all the toxic ideals that we were led to believe and having the safety to show up as your true, authentic, embodied self. This is why it is so powerful when we have the freedom to safely express our desires and be met with a "Yes! I want to do that too!" or a shame-free "I'm not interested in trying that at this time, or ever, but thank you for sharing with me what you're turned on by. It helps me to know and love you better." Even if we don't exactly know what kind of sex we desire, having the freedom and tools to know how to communicate what lights us up is deeply important as well.

One fantastic resource for discovering your sexual desires is the Erotic Blueprint, developed by Miss Jaiya, an award-winning somatic sexologist with over two decades of clinical research and client work in her repertoire. Through her work, Jaiya noticed patterns of arousal that either turned on one person or flatlined another. Because we are all so unique in our sexual desires and sexual expression, different things are going to get us each excited, and what works for one of us will not necessarily work for someone else. Maybe you crave sensuality, softness, and romance? Or maybe you get excited to explore your edges and push against what feels like a taboo?

Whatever kind of sexual person you are, these blueprints are not new boxes of confinement to enclose ourselves in but rather invitations for us to accept. Think of the blueprints as a way of personalizing your own safe space to express the fullness of your humanity. Through this self-discovery and play, we can begin to determine our true desires and liberate our own sexual expression, remembering the pieces of ourselves before they were burdened down by fear, judgment, and shame from others. It is a beautiful, holy, human thing.

Reflection

* Can you recall your first moments of sexual awakening? What did it feel like for you in your body?
* Was there ever a moment when you felt shamed or judged for your sexuality? Where did those messages of shame come from? Do you still carry those messages in your body? If so, how does that show up in your relationship with yourself, your body, your sexuality, and anyone else who you share your sexuality with?
* In what ways would you like to explore and embody your sexuality? Are there any desires that you leave unspoken? Do you feel like you can ask for what you want in the bedroom? Do you have a hesitation to ask for what you want that spills over into any other areas of your life?

Invitation

If you've ever felt disconnected from your body or afraid to let someone see your body in her fullest form, mirror work is a powerful way to change the way we see ourselves. Originally developed by self-love teacher Louise Hay, the primary focus of mirror work is to learn how to love yourself through the habitual practice of speaking love over yourself and your body. In my coaching practice, we utilize the tools of speaking affirmations combined with the practice of mirror work to go deeper into an intimate relationship with our bodies. Loving words affirm all the good things that we hold in our bodies, and when we internalize loving affirmations, they have the potential to reframe our perspective, shifting how we see ourselves and others. If you've ever longed to hear your parents, partner, or friend say something specific to you such as validating your pain, assuring you that you are taken care of, or that you are worthy or beautiful, this is an invitation to speak those things for yourself as well. If we are always seeking external validation, then we will continuously feel as though we are in a deficit. But if we learn how to cultivate and embody love for ourselves, then we can be in right relationship with ourselves and can engage in relationships with others from a place of security. This can work because you are already enough and have nothing to prove, exactly as you are. Change comes when we speak words of love over our bodies and embody love through the way that we care for our bodies and treat our bodies with reverence. Over time, we can rebuild the foundation of our relationship with our bodies and our sexuality by doing the work intentionally every day to strip away the negative messages that were given to us from a body-hostile culture.

For myself, this practice has had the most profound impact on the relationship that I have with my vulva. By spreading my legs and gazing at my vulva in the mirror, I have been able to reclaim the ability to see my body with admiration and wonder, stripping away all the derogatory ways that patriarchal culture has referenced the vulva as a source of shame and disgust. I no longer see my body as something that I give for the benefit of someone else or my sexual experiences as something that cheapens my worth, turning me into a "slut." Instead, my perspective is that my body is a powerful, beautiful, and sacred part of me and that it is an honor and privilege to be in her presence. You can take back your body and your pleasure too. If the most intimate parts of our bodies have been the target of cruel words, it can be hard to be naked in front of ourselves or another person. Stripping off the shame begins with returning to a loving, compassionate relationship with our bodies, and we find our way back to ourselves by allowing ourselves to be seen with gentle eyes. This practice can be done by people who have a penis or who are intersex as well.

When you are ready to try mirror work, start by creating an environment that makes you feel safe enough to be seen by yourself. Set the mood for yourself if that helps you feel more relaxed and comfortable. You can light candles or diffuse essential oils. Bring in flowers, lotions, massage oils, or anything else that makes you feel beautiful and sensual in your body. Find a comfortable place to lie or sit down with soft blankets or pillows holding your body. If it is not in your habit to pamper yourself in such a way, now is the time to begin; you are worthy of good things.

Once you feel comfortable, place a mirror in your view and position your body in front of it. Slowly undress and allow the layers of armor that you have metaphorically placed in protection over yourself to fall away. Take your time slowly gazing over every part of your body. It is critical that you do this act of loving self-care with gentle, soft eyes and not critical, judgmental eyes. If you find yourself critiquing all the things you dislike about your body, take a pause and come back to this exercise at a later time. Your body does not deserve to hear more unkind things said to her/him/them. Your body is worthy of being your friend and being held in a loving embrace.

As you softly gaze on all the edges, curves, folds, and lengths of your body, find something of gratitude that you can express over each part of yourself. Gaze in wonder at the beauty of your physical form. This is your home. This is your body. This is your greatest ally, and even if you don't feel close to your body at this moment, open yourself to the possibility that this gentle practice of loving gaze will slowly transform your body from a stranger to your friend. No matter the physical structure of our bodies, there is no need for us to carry around the weight of other people's judgment or shame any longer. Shame dispels when brave stories are compassionately shared in safe spaces. Allow yourself to be a safe person for your body.

Chapter 9

The Intuitive Voice

What we give voice to, we give life to.

Giana was free-spirited and unafraid to conform to the expectations of those around her. Creative, earthy, and unafraid of the unconventional, she didn't mind walking down the path less traveled. When we started working together and I learned more of her story, she shared with me how her body would shut down when she wanted to be sexual with her partner. She wasn't raised in purity culture or religion, so we got curious about her past and began to unravel some of the stories her body was holding onto. We discovered old memories she had of being locked in a room as a child and how that experience left her feeling out of control and needing to control other aspects of her life. As a result, she felt locked up in her body. She went on to tell me how it became a family joke that she would always find a way to pick the lock and escape from her room. "Giana," I told her, "do you realize that you had the key in your hands all along?" Even as a child, she knew how to free herself. My job, as her embodiment coach, was simply to remind her of this truth and share with her some skills so that she could unlock her own freedom and healing. Reframing this revelation brought Giana not only back into her body but back into reclaiming her voice as well.

Trusting the Voice Within

Our own internal voice is the key, and through intuition, emotion, and body sensations, our voice speaks to us all day long if we listen to its wisdom. Our bodies speak to us of hunger, how fast we can safely run down a hill, who is dangerous, and what it feels like to be living in alignment with our integrity. As we've already explored, systemic body-based oppression and religion can disrupt the relationship we have with our bodies by teaching us to mistrust and ignore them. This doesn't only impact our relationship with our bodies; it silences our inner voice so that we no longer know how to trust ourselves. When we abandon our inner compass because we've been taught to distrust our bodies by abusive parents, manipulative partners, or unethical religious leaders, we can experience self-betrayal, anxiety, and strong feelings of disorientation. If you are not sure which voice in your head is your own, begin to cultivate your relationship with your body. The practice of Embodied Questioning for Truth can be a helpful tool as well. Notice when your gut speaks to you; this is the voice of your inner intuition. By rebuilding a familiarity with your intuition, you can repair trust and the lines of communication between you and your body. Sometimes this process will feel safest when you remove yourself from unhealthy relationships with people in your life, but it is not always necessary. Oftentimes we can heal and still maintain balanced relationships with others. But in order to do so, we must establish embodied boundaries so that we have the space to figure out a balance between our own internal voice and the influence of others.

The Power of Reclaiming Our Voice, Our Body, and Our Autonomy

Reclaiming our voices and advocating for ourselves begins when we have the courage to speak up even if we are still afraid. This skill can feel threatening at first, but once we begin listening to our bodies and honor their needs, we learn that we cannot silence the voice within any longer. What would it look like to fully *inhabit* our bodies and our voices, instead of using them to perform or adapt for someone else?

Connecting with our embodied voice impacts so much more than our relationship with just our bodies. It also influences how we show up in relationships with other people. When I was younger, more concerned with the comfort of others and trying to be the "good girl," I didn't know how to embody my voice. I also didn't know how to listen to the voice within my body. As a child, I remember being taught not to ask for food or water when visiting other people's homes and instead to wait until it had been offered to me. The message I internalized through this teaching was that it was more important for me to sit quietly and wait than to advocate for my needs. The social graces of politeness were more important than caring for my body. Later in life this evolved into me not knowing how to advocate for myself in many different social situations but most importantly my romantic and sexual relationships as a teenager and young adult. Relationships at this point in our lives are often messy and unscripted, but for those who are raised to be quiet and polite, it can be especially challenging to learn how and when to use your voice to stand up for yourself.

Thankfully, somatic literacy taught me how to cultivate my voice by coming back to my body and writing a new pathway into my nervous system. Over time I began to replace the teachings of my youth as I learned to take up space in my body. Where I was once afraid to show my shoulders for fear of judgment, I began to wear clothing that made me feel like my most authentic, embodied, and joy-filled self. Instead of feeling like I had to silence my needs for the sake of politeness, I learned how to advocate for my own needs in a way that honored my whole self while also extending the same curiosity onto others. Most importantly, I invited my whole body to wake back up with me as a resistance to any system of oppression or ideology that told me not to fully inhabit my body. I rejected the notion that living out the fullness of my humanity might be a "stumbling block" to others. I chose instead to believe that my body is overflowing with goodness and wholeness and that I don't need to silence her or force her to conform to any patriarchal, colonial standard of expectation and performance.

This process of finding and embodying my own voice by listening to the voice within influenced every aspect of my life. Learning how to embody my voice gave me the ability to negotiate salaries and advocate for a healthy work-life balance in my professional life. Learning how to embody my voice gave me the ability to better articulate my needs, my traumas, and my boundaries to those in my personal life. Learning to embody my voice helped me walk away from my people-pleasing tendencies so that I would leave abusive relationships. Learning to embody my voice gave me the courage to identify harmful relationships and practices that do not align with who I want to be.

The powerful thing about reclamation is that when we come back into right relationship with our bodies, our voice, and our whole selves, it will undoubtedly make an impact on those around us. These ripples of influence can be felt through the interpersonal connections we have as well. When I am able to see myself and my body through more compassionate, curious, tender, and trauma-informed eyes, then I am able to see others and their bodies in a more human way as well. Likewise, when we dehumanize ourselves and allow the guilt, shame, and self-hatred to seep into our bones, we will inevitably impose the same level of judgment and violence onto others; the two are always interconnected. This is why being in right relationship with our bodies is so critical—and such a revolutionary act. When my clients come to this same realization, it is powerful to see the profound impact it makes on their relationships with their bodies and everyone else they interact with. I have watched in wonder and awe as people have awakened for the first time to their inner power, their sacred knowing, and their ability to heal from the inside out. By listening to her body, Amanda learned how to listen to the red flags her body was waving for her, honor herself, and walk away from an abusive marriage. Winnie was able to notice her people-pleasing habits and begin to advocate for her needs and her embodied boundaries. Kay was able to realize the ways that they had forced their body to be something they were not and open more for a more authentic, embodied gender expression. Our voices are always within us, waiting to be set free.

Embodied Voice and Interconnected Advocacy

Noticing the ways we have been silenced in our personal lives and coming back to reembody our voice creates ripples that affect far more than just ourselves. The path of liberation is capable of ushering in a more collective liberation for everyone. The power of embodying our voice does so much more than teach us how to advocate more effectively for our needs; it also teaches us how to stand with and amplify the voices of others who are being silenced by the regime of body-based oppression all around us. This is where solidarity and interconnectedness flows as we move from self-actualization to community actualization. When we reclaim our shared humanity and leverage our voices, our privilege, our education, then we can use every other resource in our arsenal to ensure that no one is left behind. Relationship is the only antidote for the isolation and pain of loneliness. Reciprocity is the only antidote for all the ways that the systems of classism, capitalism, and hierarchies of body-based oppression have broken our relationships and distanced us from one another.

For this work to be effective, we must remember that there is no one among us who is voiceless—only voices that are being silenced or overlooked. In church spaces, I would often hear these words spoken over me—that I was a "voice for the voiceless"—when the reality is that no one in this entire world is truly voiceless. Instead, there are forces at work within the systemic framework that silences or over-shadows the voices of those who have been pushed into the margins. When this happens, we must push back against any kind of hierarchy of superiority or silencing. As advocates and laborers for justice and truth, we must be cautious to tend to the voices of everyone and ensure that we are not enabling the erasure of others. I learned the power of advocacy with my boots on the ground in my local commu-nity, in the neon lights of the world's most dehumanizing red-light districts, in the dusty slums of villages and in the halls of parliamen-tary power. One thing I have learned from these years of collective community mobilization is that the work of an advocate is to listen carefully and leverage the platform as a megaphone for others.

What Robin Wall Kimmerer calls "the covenant of reciprocity" is so vital to doing justice work or decolonizing efforts in a good and healing way. Every relationship must be built on a deep knowing of one another, and the parties involved must come to the table with a posture of curiosity and humility. For our efforts for embodiment and justice to be successful, we must be willing to lay down our rights in exchange for our responsibilities to one another. We must walk together, at whatever pace is necessary for no one to be left behind. With this value as the foundation of our work, my friends and colleagues have often asked me to stand next to them, before them as a shield or behind them as a backup. In moments where they needed to leverage the voice of someone else as a support, we found that together our two voices were louder than one.

Sometimes that looks like standing against injustice and the racial profiling of my Indigenous sister by a hotel clerk. Sometimes that has looked like bringing forward the written testimonies and stories of undocumented human trafficking survivors to mainstream media. Sometimes it is passing the mic by sharing the voices of others in this book. *Every time* it is remembering that leveraging voice is not about us—but amplifying the voices of the unheard. An important part of being an advocate is recognizing when we need to get out of the way so that people can have the space to advocate for themselves. In this process of listening, we will often learn that the most pressing needs of others might not be what we thought they needed—and this is critical to the health of our movements and more importantly, our relationships.

I learned this lesson most profoundly when I worked among the women who were trafficked behind the glass windows of the redlight district that bordered South and North Korea's demilitarized zone. Far from any major cities, their bodies were rented by primarily male tourists who would travel by coach bus to meet them. Here, sex work was not a choice but an entrapment. To service men more effectively, the women behind the windows had every tooth of their front row of teeth pulled to give more space in their mouths to perform oral sex on paying customers. Those who managed to find their way out of this horrific situation faced costly dental bills and trauma counseling while in recovery. When I was given the opportunity to advocate for their voices in South Korea's Congress, this was the message that they wanted me to share, as it was critical for their recovery homes to receive more financial support for dental work. In the halls of power, leveraging a rhinestone crown and satin sash, I found that their voices were indeed able to speak through mine. As an outside collaborator from a different culture, I could not have known this need of theirs had there not been the connection of relationship already established. If I had come in with my own ideas of what the women needed, it would have been the wrong thing. Listening to and valuing everyone's voices made all the difference.

This happens daily much closer to home as well—in fact, within the walls of my very home and the life that I share with my partner and my children. As a parent, I have my own hopes and dreams for my children, just as my parents and grandparents had their own hopes and dreams for me, I am sure. But being a parent does not mean that I own my children; they do not belong to me. They are their own people. They have their own ways of viewing and experiencing the world. They have their own knowledge and wisdom held in their bodies. They have their own connection to spirituality. And they experience this all apart from me. What their lives turn out to be is not for me to decide, dictate, or have expectations for.

My role, as their parent, is to help them discover their voices for themselves, to learn how to embody their own autonomy and to embrace the wisdom that comes to them from within. My role, as their parent, is to get myself out of their way. My role, as their parent, is to help them learn to listen to the voice that comes from within them and distinguish it from all the voices swirling around them that seek to persuade them for their own agendas and goals. My role, as their parent, is to help them learn to rise and see the good in themselves, in a way that simultaneously spills over and allows them to see the good in everyone else as well. This is the power of bringing our embodiment into every relationship we hold; it creates ripples that extend far beyond ourselves and has the power to profoundly shift our lived experiences for generations to come. When you reclaim your voice, your body, and your whole self, it is not only a defiant act of resistance against body-based oppression; it also paves the way for collective liberation for everyone else around you. This is why your journey to embodiment is so critical. It's about more than just you. It's about us all.

Reflection

Connect with your body in a way that is meaningful to you. Ground yourself in the moment and approach the conversation with your body with openness and curiosity. We are here to learn, not to pass judgment, criticism, or shame over ourselves for the answers we find.

Ask your body's intuitive wisdom to show you any of the ways that you may have adapted to make yourself small or silenced your authentic voice for the comfort of others. Go deeper and ask where this comes from? Is it in an effort for safety? Did you learn it from others who modeled a similar behavior? Can you recall a memory when speaking up caused you to be the target of escalated violence or aggression? Have you ever experienced pushback for speaking your authentic voice?

On the flip side, maybe you didn't silence your authentic voice but rather took on a voice that was not your own. What does this voice sound like? Whose voice are you imitating? What made you abandon your authentic voice for the voice of someone else? Did it make you feel safer? More powerful? If you step closer and peel back the layers of why you took on this new voice, what would you find? Is there something underneath this new voice that is protecting a tender part of you that you don't want others to see?

Sit with whatever your body shows you through this exercise. Give yourself space to reflect on and process whatever comes up through this. Journal, take a walk, or turn on some music and move through the emotions that arise as you reflect and dig deeper. Remember to not throw yourself into shame for whatever you find. We all have very good reasons for doing what we do, and it usually points back to a desire for safety, belonging, and connection.

Invitation

If you discover something through this embodiment exercise that you seek to let go of, write it down on a piece of paper and tear it up or burn it. While this process may be largely symbolic, it allows our body to walk through the motions of letting something go. Write your affirmations or do an embodied meditation to welcome in your new intentions to create a new pathway forward for your body.

Chapter 10

Embodiment as a Spiritual Practice

There is a whole universe of magic living in your body, as you breathe in each moment filled with the wonder and mystery of the incomprehensible divine.

Spirituality is such an interesting thing to write about. How does one even begin to describe that which is indescribable? What language do we give for an experience that cannot be captivated by words? How do we logically engage with something that defies all logic and leaves us standing in the mystery of that which is beyond human understanding? To me, spirituality is essential to life. Life in and of itself is spirituality in the way that I know it. But that does not mean that everyone views life and spirituality in the same way. And truthfully, that's part of why I love it so much.

From atheism to mysticism to fundamental religion or a blend of it all, spirituality is diverse and fascinating, with everyone experiencing it in a different way. Spirituality exists in a vast, expansive realm that cannot be fully understood or explained. When I asked my online community what words they used to describe their own spiritual experiences, I was deeply moved by the breadth and depth of what was shared. I heard names of God, Goddess, god, Universe, Spirit, Source, Creator, Divinity, the All-Knowing-Infinite, Universal Self, Beloved, Mother God, Mother Earth, Interconnected, As Above So Below, Truth, Love, Transcendent, Mystery, Collective Consciousness, Nature, Third Eye, Pachamama, Great Designer, Sophia, Sacred Knowing Within, Energy, Presence, Siila, Core, Roots, Guiding Light, the Mother—and the list goes on and on. This limitless expansiveness, while strikingly different from the evangelical preaching of certainty that I experienced in my youth, brings me such peace and comfort in my spiritual life today.

My spiritual life has been in a constant state of evolution for the past number of years. Even now I regularly receive messages from strangers who once heard me preach from platforms and pulpits who are now asking if I still love Jesus and live for him. And I can't blame them for their curiosity. I am not the same person I was five years ago, ten years ago, or fifteen years ago; for this I am grateful. My spiritual growth and exploration are important to me. I do not want to ever to get a place in my life where I am stagnant in my faith, my beliefs, or my understandings; I desire to be continuously challenged and presented with new information. I long to grow outwards into a wider and more expansive view of the world around me.

Many people still in church view those who are deconstructing their faith as backsliders. Those who are questioning or going in a different direction may not be seen as "real" Christians anymore. And in some ways, yes: we are choosing to go a different direction. After the events of the last few years, I can barely think of anyone who hasn't had their faith transformed in some way or another by what has unfolded on a global and interpersonal scale. Personally, I began publicly wrestling with the ways that the church upheld body-based hierarchies of power and oppression back in 2011. I was outspoken in my community groups and from the pulpit as I noticed the way the church treated women. I watched the way that stained-glass ceilings held back women in churches around the world, and I read Jesus' teachings on equality and inclusion. When I spoke on the TEDx stage in 2016 and dug into the intersections of faith and feminism, I did so by exposing harmful, patriarchal theology in contrast to the early church's egalitarian roots.

This TED conference took place only one week before the 2016 US election. What unfolded over the next few years brought us all to a place of deep reflection and public wrestling with the influence that the church had on political, economic, and social events. I witnessed the ways that the church failed us through its allegiance to Trump and the radicalization of white supremacist subcultures connected to the religious right. I listened to Christian leaders promoting xeno-phobic rhetoric to build a wall with the intent of keeping others out rather than welcoming the refugee and the foreigner in, as we hear the scriptures say again and again. I watched as millions took to the streets to decry institutionalized racism and violence, unapolo-getically pleading for Black lives to matter, while many pastors and congregants stayed within their homes and denounced critical race theory and simultaneously uplifted thin blue stripes on their Ameri-can and Canadian flags. I saw Christians legislating violence against trans children who bear the image of God in their transformation, forgetting that Jesus himself crossed all biological understanding to be both fully human and fully God—a transformation that many of us still do not understand to this day. I listened as priests spoke of their support of the horrific Indian residential school system, declar-ing that good was done in these death camps, even as thousands of unmarked graves were uncovered on church property and survivor stories revealed how the government and church worked together

to take Indigenous children from their homes through forced assimilation and forced conversion. I watched as those who I had once
sat in church with refused to wear masks in a pandemic to protect
the immunocompromised among us when we had all been raised in
Sunday school to hold the value of protecting "the least of these"
and defend the most vulnerable among us. I watched in horror as
every core value of loving our neighbor and doing good to those who
harmed us was disregarded and tossed aside by those who once pro-
claimed the same faith as I.

I realized that I could no longer align myself with such communities anymore. It was not that my values, my theology, or my worldview had changed; it was that somewhere along the line, the people
who taught me my Sunday school classes were no longer embodying the values that they were teaching through sermons and flan-
nelgraph. I could no longer find Jesus within the stained-glass walls
of the church; at some point, he had left to march alongside the
people in their wounding, their grief, their mourning, and their cries
for justice. So, at some point, I followed him out the door, and I left.

Deconstructing Faith and Reconstructing Embodiment

Coming back to my body allowed me to notice where I was being
swept up by institutions that didn't embody my core values. When I
silenced all the noise of the other voices imposed on me from somewhere else, I was left with the still, small voice of deep inner knowing within—a voice that I believe connects me to a spiritual source
greater than myself. With this new revelation I was able to see and
experience how much more vast and embodied spirituality is than I
was taught as a child.

I began to realize that I didn't need someone to tell me what
God was like; I could have a spiritual experience and relationship for

myself. I began to see the Bible as less of the idol that it has become and more of a library of written works transcribed by those who had their own encounters with unexplained spirituality. I saw the Bible as a tool to understand spirituality better rather than the final word and authority on what the human experience should be like. Some may call this heretical, but the more I study church history, the more I realize it is the heretics who have taught us, shaped us, and expanded our understanding of what God is capable of, not the ones who claim, "The Bible is clear about . . . ." Through this exploration I found the vast, expansive experience of spirituality in my body, the one place I was taught not to look.

What Christianity Got Wrong

If I were to write an exhaustive list of all the things Christianity has gotten wrong throughout the ages, this book would have no ending. And this is not the goal. We all know of the ways that Christianity, as an institution, has sided with political forces when it was supposed to be about the power of love and not the love of power. We all know of the ways that Christianity has sided with violence and bloodshed when it was supposed to be about radical inclusion and turning the other cheek. We all know of the ways that Christianity has sided with colonization when it was supposed to be about washing the feet of one another and breaking bread at the table of kinship. We all know of the ways that Christianity has torn down queer beauty in the name of traditional family values and weaponized fear over the imago dei in us all. But for a faith tradition built around the incarnation of the Divine and a God who became human, Christianity has forgotten much of its humanity and the mystery that exists within spirituality.

In my experience, the physicality of the human body is deeply spiritual. The dirt of the earth is deeply spiritual. The air in our lungs is deeply spiritual. The connections and kinship between all things are deeply spiritual. The things of our lives that exist in the realm of the sacred, spiritual, and holy do not have to be distant, sanitized, or superior for them to be profound. Our spiritual experiences can begin within our own bodies and our relationships with all things. One such example of this juxtaposition between the spiritual and the physical is the deeply sacred experience of bringing new life into the world. As one who is in love with birth, I will never stop being captivated by the birth story of Mary and Jesus. While we may never agree on whether Jesus was the embodiment of God in human form or not, the historical person of Jesus Christ still holds wonder and mystery for me. I do not know exactly what happened in that little town of Bethlehem, but I have a feeling that the night was far from silent.

After standing at the bedside of many laboring women and bringing three of my own babies earthside, I can tell you that birth is anything but silent, clean, or serene. Birth is a powerfully profound human experience. Never have I witnessed a person in a more primal, raw, and human state than when one is actively in the midst of giving birth. There is nothing polite or sanitized about it. Everything we are taught about how to behave in public falls away, and all that remains is the animalistic side of our humanity. I have witnessed people in the labor of birth moaning, groaning, and roaring their babies earthside. There is blood and mucus, stretching and tearing, and a new life entering the world as an old life sheds away. No one who has ever witnessed birth has walked away from the experience unchanged in some way.

For Jesus to be a living breathing human who entered the world through blood, sweat, tears, and amniotic fluid tells me that any sanitized version of Christianity that is more concerned with upholding doctrine and political agenda has forgotten the humanity in spirituality's roots. We do not have to put on our Sunday best to be whole and good. We do not have to sanitize or wipe away our humanity in order to embrace the holy. Reclaiming our whole selves, even in the midst of our mess, is a profoundly human and holy experience that opens us up to view our bodies, as well as the bodies of everyone else around us, with more compassion. When we feel safe enough to fully inhabit our bodies again and bring our nervous system back from trauma, we can begin to see the world with gentler eyes, because we've understood the ways that trauma influences our reactions and can break or heal our relationships.

By embracing our whole selves, even the parts of ourselves that still need healing, we can begin the journey back home. We can reclaim it immediately, the very same day that we choose to do better by loving more. And isn't that the point of spirituality? Isn't God the definition of love? Our experience on earth can bridge all the divides that were broken by the loss of reciprocity. Our spirituality is something that can be experienced, lived out, as close to us as the very air that fills our lungs in each breath. The blood and the sweat, the dirt and the brokenness teach us so much more about finding the sacred amid our humanity. These are the moments in which embodiment and spirituality intertwine. This is where I see the body as good, powerfully profound, and inherently holy.

When we live our lives this way—breaking bread together, standing against the marginalization of all people, and embodying the teachings of nonviolence and compassion to everyone we encounter—we find that there is so much beauty yet to be experienced within us and our relationships. We do not dismantle oppressive systems of power through force; we choose love instead, as it is far more powerful to embody our values through daily life than to impose them with the sword. The revolution starts within us—within our hearts, within our bodies, within the way we view the world and interact with one another. So we choose to show up, consistently and compassionately, loving each other through radical embodiment and transformational justice, knowing that healing broken relationships through the covenant of reciprocity is the goal.

When we remember our humanity beyond party lines, state lines, and church aisles, shifting our worldview from "us versus them" to a relationship with faces, names, lives, and stories, powerful shifts can happen. This does not mean that we have to engage with some- one who is choosing to be actively harmful or perpetuating oppres- sion. Sometimes we cannot keep an abusive person in our lives, and we have to come to the difficult decision of wishing them well and letting their path go a different way from ours. But in our appeal for accountability or our work for justice, we cannot dehumanize another person. Dehumanizing breaks the relationship and the cov- enant of reciprocity, just like injustice does. We must always work for the reconciliation of all relationships, whenever possible. Relation- ships change everything. Relationships change the world.

Making Space for an Embodied Relationship with Spirituality in Daily Life

Reframing our very humanity as a spiritual experience extends an invitation to view every moment of our lives as something divine. We don't need to purchase anything to connect with our spirituality. We do not need doctorates, diplomas, or letters behind our names to prove our connection with the divine. We simply need to listen to the still, small voice that speaks to us from within and connects us to everything else that has ever existed.

Where my upbringing was built on doctrine and theology as dictated by others, my spiritual life today includes a limitless understanding and relationship with God that can be accessed by contemplative experiences of the world around me and within me.

Sometimes this looks like being out in nature or belly laughs shared with my closest friends until we are all rolling around on the floor. It feels like fresh morning dew, or the golden pink sunset painted across the coastal mountain range on the longest day of the year. It tastes like resonance when I meet a stranger and connect on a level that makes each of us feel a little less alone in the world, even if we never speak beyond that fleeting moment of solidarity. It smells like a fresh newborn baby, all swaddled and warm in my arms, holding the promise of hope and possibility. And yes, spirituality and holiness are even present in the few final moments at the bedside of a loved one as they split away from us into the next realm. Or the silent prayers of my heart as I lie on the floor of my bedroom, sobbing, because I simply cannot make sense of the world around me, and my grief feels almost too much to bear. These are the moments of holiness, when heaven touches earth; God, Spirit, or Source in the midst of everything, interconnecting me with everything else that has ever existed.

Reflection

* What words, sounds, or visuals would you use to most accurately describe your relationship with spirituality?
* How do these experiences feel in your body?
* What could it look like to embody your spirituality within you as you experience it?

Invitation

Journal, meditate on, or move through your discoveries as you reflect on the ways you have encountered and engaged with spirituality. Keep space in each experience to remember that your journey can evolve and flow as you grow through life.

Chapter 11

In Right Relationship

We do not achieve liberation on our own, it is always through inter-dependence and right relationship that we come home to our bodies and each other.

What does right relationship mean to you? I asked this question of a client when we were working together a few years ago, and she paused to consider something she had never reflected on before. She looked up at me with wide eyes, "What do you mean, 'right relationship'?" We were talking in the context of listening to the signs of her body trying to speak to her (high anxiety, digestive issues, relationship conflicts) and learning to slow down and savor, being grounded in the moment. She had been flying through her life at maximum speed; everything and everyone she encountered served some kind of purpose for her, and by her own account, she was the person who wanted to get "a bang for her buck."

But her body needed something different. Her body needed to slow down and savor, to eat slow-cooked, nourishing foods rather than fast-food express. Her relationships needed time to develop, and her therapy sessions needed periods of reflection. The mindset she had is one that is very common for many of us; our fast-paced world has conditioned us to look for quick fixes: "buy this product," "read this book," "do this thirty-day challenge." We view our bodies as projects, and if we can just unlock the key as to which resource we need, then we will be "fixed." But how would our lives change if we interacted with our bodies as relationships for us to nurture rather than projects for us to fix? How would our lives change if we applied the mindset of relationship to all things, from the coffee we drink to the clothes we wear to the people we meet?

Viewing the world through the lens of relationship moves us from things that serve us to a reflection on and deep respect for the embodied stories we each hold and the interconnected ways in which we depend on one another. When we treat people and things as resources, we cheapen the potential of our knowing relationship. We rush from one thing to another, and we don't give ourselves time to integrate, absorb, reflect, or transform. In this case, my former client was consuming a large amount of information from the deconstructing faith community: attending conferences, listening to podcasts, reading books, and going to therapy. The amount of information she was taking in on a weekly basis was impressive. Yet without slowing down to integrate each new idea she learned, her body was unable to digest and embody these new ideas. She was bypassing the process of moving information from head knowledge into deeply integrated and embedded body knowledge. And this is something I know to be true of many of us: if we do not integrate the new ideas we learn, then they will not become embodied within us. There is a huge difference between what we understand cognitively in our minds and what we know deep within our bodies. This is where knowledge evolves into wisdom and lived experience. And like many things in life, lived experience cannot be rushed; it must be embodied.

For this transformation to happen within us, we need to return to right relationship with all things. We need to see ideas as things or beings to be in relationship with, rather than resources for us to extract from. Right relationship, or reciprocity, is the core value that changes our perception and interaction with everything we encounter in this life. Reciprocity: this word has become my guiding light in everything I do. Its definition is the practice of exchanging things with others for mutual benefit. While the dictionary categorizes this as a noun, deep in my body I feel this is a verb. This action of mutual caregiving and reciprocal flourishing is living, breathing, and active. In fact, it is the very thing that keeps us alive.

Years of watching my mother nurturing her vegetable garden was like witnessing an embodiment of reciprocity with the land. In late February, the tiny seedlings would find their way into little mounds of soil, tucked neatly into fiber pots and under the warm glow of grow lights in a shelf in our living room. She'd mist them daily and speak kind words over each of them, encouraging their growth and resilience as they came into our world. Eventually, once their stocks became sturdy and our wet Pacific Northwest climate became less cool, she would transfer them into raised plots of land on a neighboring farm: each in neat little rows, standing side by side, with a wooden marker at the end of each line that proudly displayed their name for all to see. With dedication she would return to the soil every single day. She would weed, water, and wait, weed, water, and wait some more. She knew where to go to harvest the ocean's seaweed after every rough winter storm, and she would lay out each long, wavy piece of kelp onto her garden beds to return the ocean vegetation to the earth, filling her soil with nutrient-dense vitamins that would decompose and renew through the little plants that would one day sustain us.

Eventually as the days got longer and the warmth of the summer sun began to coax the tiny plants out of their earthy cocoons, they began to reach high toward the light with fervor and tenacity. The growth we would see in such a short amount of time was outstanding! Tiny little seedlings who once would barely withstand the gentle mist of a water bottle were now towering over my head, branches laden with long cucumbers, ripe red tomatoes, juicy peaches, and deeply buried potatoes. Some vegetables were always lost to the little creatures of the garden, but there was always enough to share. By harvest time our kitchen counters were overflowing! And you could never come visit my mother's house without leaving with some kind of zucchini or a bag of golden berries being tucked away into your purse or sweater pocket. This bounty of locally grown, hand-harvested vegetables was her love letter to us. She fed her family nourishing food when we were growing alongside the vegetable plants ourselves, and she nourished her own mental health by breathing in the fresh air and digging her hands into the earth's rich soil every day. There was a balanced dance of give and take that culminated in a delicious, tossed garden salad at our family dinner table on those long, warm summer nights. Late in the winter season, her long days spent digging in the dirt, under the summer sun, continued to pay off as we sipped spiced spoonfuls of elderberry syrup to keep the winter illness out of our bodies.

In each of these moments, my relationship with the fruit and vegetables on my dinner plate felt different than the ones I picked up at the grocery store. I knew these plants. I saw where they came from. I witnessed their birth, their growth, and their coming of age. Eating their goodness and integrating their existence within me was always a deep, reflective moment of gratitude. I savored each bite of those vegetables differently, and their flavors danced in a different way on my tongue. I meditate on this reciprocity that we held with the plants, and its implications often through my work, life, and embodiment practice. How would life change for each of us if we experienced all things in our daily lives with the same posture of gratitude and mutual benefit? If we gave back to what we took in a way that ensured mutual flourishing, even long after our encounters had faded away? If we left people, places, things, and nonhuman kin better than how we found them, in a way that spurred on the kind of right relationship that we wish to see experienced for all one day in the world? Doing all things in the spirit of reciprocity has become a spiritual practice for me.

In this way plants, and not only my mother's garden vegetables, are some of my greatest teachers on embodiment and reciprocity. If you were to come over to my home for a visit (and I hope one day you do), you would find an apartment-sized houseplant jungle in suburban Vancouver. Through my relationship with these green beings, I have learned to be in a relationship of reciprocity with plants. I learn about each individual one, what their species needs to thrive, how much sunlight to give them, their favorite place to stand in our apartment, when to water them, when to fertilize, when to prune back and cut away the dead things so they can release and grow, and when to cheer them on as they unfurl a new leaf. My plants have taught me that growing goodness takes time and when we speak to living things with kindness, they grow with more vitality. As I nurture and care for these green beings in right relationship, they care for me in return, giving clean oxygen back into our home and providing a sanctuary of relaxing oasis so that our mental stress can lift when we return to this space at the end of each day. The relationships I hold with my plants have impacted me so profoundly that they often seep into my conversations with clients—so much so that one client of mine and I will often relate caring for ourselves as caring for the basic needs of our houseplants, ensuring that we too get adequate sunlight, fresh air, hydration, and rest. Yes, even houseplants know that there is a time to rest and recharge when the growing season is done, and we return to winter.

One of the ways we become disembodied is that we forget that we are part of nature. Our bodies come from nature and will one day return to nature. We are cyclical as the earth's seasons are cyclical and the moon's phases are cyclical. When we reject nature, we reject ourselves and disembody from the wisdom we hold within. Many of the world's creation stories, including the book of Genesis, claim that humanity was born of soil: made of the dirt, mud, and clay, born of the very thing we often despise and seek to sanitize ourselves from. Ever since the advent of electricity, our tech-based lives have been distanced from the interconnected ecosystem upon which all life depends. We stopped thinking about where our food comes from, how we need the recycled oxygen from trees to breathe, that our quality of life depends on the quality of the water, both in our bodies and in the world around us. We forget about our relationship and kinship to all things. And we lose out on so much when we treat people and the earth like resources for our benefit, rather than relationships to grow in, care for, and cherish.

When we return to this lens of viewing the world, we see the interconnectedness that exists between us, the sovereignty that each species holds within themselves, and the ways in which our being weaves an ecosystem of interdependence among one another. Through my ceremonial adoption into local Indigenous communities, I have consistently heard Indigenous teachings refer to the natural world as nonhuman kin, including everything from fungi and cedar to salmon and sasquatch, emphasizing the familial relationship we hold with all living things, regardless of species or DNA. This covenant of reciprocity holds the world in balance, and yet humans would rather send billionaire investments into space than return to what has been broken by the loss of right relationship here on our home planet and within our own bodies.

I see tiny sermons and life lessons of the meaning of reciprocity often, everywhere in nature, and some of the best lessons are taught to me by the littlest teachers who show me the way. Reciprocity honors the beingness that is inherent within all things and transforms our understanding of an object, person, or idea from a resource for us to extract and consume to something for us to know deeply, intimately, and personally—to be in relationship with.

Think about the things you cherish in your life. I'm sure there are people, places, objects, and memories that hold significant value to you. Maybe you have an item that was given to you by a loved one or a family heirloom that had been made by a great-grandmother and passed down to you through the generations of your family. I have precious items like this. Jewelry that was made and gifted to me by a survivor of sex trafficking whom I worked with while in Thailand. A quilt that was hand-stitched for me by a dear friend from Ottawa. River rocks that sit on my altar that were collected by the tiny hands of my children while they played in a winding stream near my house. Some of these items are mundane, while others could be replaced by something identical at a local department store. But the stories they all carry are precious and irreplaceable. More importantly, the people and land they came from are precious and irreplaceable.

It is through this understanding that I became committed to purchasing only ethically sourced, sustainable, and fair-trade goods whenever possible. This led me to awaken to a whole new community that was thriving all around me. A community built on the interconnected weaving of slow living, earth-respecting practices, handmade goodness, and deeply known relationships. Before long I had someone I knew who could supply all the goods that my family used regularly that I was unable to make myself. Mel made the clothing that I would wear on my body when I woke for the morning each day. Karen crafted the balms, sprays, and lotions that would hydrate my body and cleanse my skin. LeiLani formulated the makeup that gave me a boost of glow on a tired day. Jackie beaded the earrings that adorned my ears and provided me with a source of inspiration. Jessica filed, stamped, engraved, and polished the small pendant of gold that rose and fell with each breath as it sat across my neck. Casey and Dakota printed the sweater that kept my body warm and spoke of my values for decolonization with the world. The Red Yao women from an Indigenous tribe in China crafted the rice shampoo bars that cleansed my hair every time I stepped into the shower. Christine grew the herbs that were hand blended into the teas that I would sip at the end of the night.

Together, we wove an intricate web of human relationships with respect for each other and reverence for our nonhuman kin of the natural world, from which all the elements for our daily products were harvested and sustained. And through each purchase, we knew, deep in our bodies, that we were not only receiving an object that had been lovingly created with intention and care; we were also making it possible for our friends to put food on their tables and clothes on the backs of their own children in a new, locally based economy that didn't continue to line the pockets of big-name corporate CEOs who would never step foot into our neighborhoods or care if the workers who harvested their raw materials were paid a fair living wage in a safe environment that left enough for Mother Earth to survive, flourish, and renew. My relationship to these items is different when I value where they come from, the ethics in which they were made, and the memories of the people and places they represent. All these items that I hold dear, while merely objects, represent to me a relationship of reciprocity: where there is giving and receiving, where there is mutual care, where there is respect and understanding, and where there is a desire for mutual flourishing. When we approach our relationship with everything that exists through this lens rather than the lens of resource and commodity, everything we see in the world expands to let more imagination and light in.

Right Relationship versus Domination

The land where I live is surrounded by lush, coniferous rainforest. Our home is thirty minutes from the city, thirty minutes from the mountains, and thirty minutes from the ocean. Outdoor adventures are easy to access, and my children have attended school in the forest since they were tiny toddlers standing among the ancient cedar trees. Now they know every trail in the woods where they grew up. They can tell me the life cycle of the salmon and the salamander; they know where the beavers work and not to disrupt the beds of clay on the river's edge, so as to not harm the fish as they spawn. In the winter months they learn the crunch of the snow, and in the spring, they know to watch for the rise of the waters as they wait for the green leaves and juicy berries of the forest to return. They also learn how to listen to their bodies as they climb the welcoming limbs of each swooping cedar tree that offers its branches toward the tiny humans who seek to challenge their capacities or ascend higher into an imaginary game full of woodland faeries, falcons, fawns, and other creatures that call the forest their home. Countless hours spent under the canopy of conifers taught my children how to discern when to take another hydrating drink of water, whether their toes were cold inside their boots, or if their bodies told them it was time to put on another pair of mittens to keep their little hands safe from the West Coast rain or winter snow. The forest is our unspoken teacher, and the lessons she imparted to my children come from an ancient wisdom that no amount of research could ever share from the pages of a textbook; it could only be grasped through right relationship and seeing our world from within the interconnectedness that aligns with our own bodies.

With this wisdom embodied within her, my daughter told us decidedly one day that trees belong to themselves. We were driving through the Fraser Valley of British Columbia, discussing the ever-rising real estate prices in our area (a common topic of discussion for all millennial parents). I shared about how some of the top landowners in the world are the British royal family, the Catholic Church, and the McDonald's corporation. The response to my statement came immediately and confidently from the backseat of our car: "And the trees, Mama! You forgot: the trees belong to themselves." Her words sunk deep into my soul as I let them echo through the space we shared in our car, driving the winding roads of Highway 1 through the Sumas Valley. She was right. The trees belonged to themselves. And when the era of colonization took over the very lands we were driving along, humans forgot the truth that my four-year-old daughter reminded me on that day: *the trees belonged to themselves.*

This ancient truth stood in contrast with the legality of the land we drove along. In 1871, my province of British Columbia became part of the Dominion of Canada. All the lands and ocean that stretched across the northern west coast of what had previously been known as Turtle Island came under the rule of the British empire, and rather than being viewed as nonhuman kin for the Indigenous people to share relationship with, the land and ocean were transformed into rich resources of lumber for building a new colonized country, fish for feeding a new immigrant population, and fur pelts for declaring a mark of status for the English upper class. The humans came to extract from the land rather than to know and be with the land. And this relationship shift came with dire consequences.

In the fall of 2021, the very road that I had been driving along with my family just a few months before was nearly indistinguishable from aerial views above. A massive storm, increasing the heavy rainfall that this region is traditionally known for, began to fill the nearby rivers and Sumas Prairie that wound through a nutrient-dense valley that is known as BC's largest agricultural town. The entire valley flooded, causing billions in damage and catastrophic loss to both human and nonhuman lives. Our entire province was declared to be in a state of emergency as highways were washed out, bridges broke, herds of cattle disappeared, and homes filled with water; the entire region became a lake, cut off from the rest of the country. But as this crisis happened all around us, the land taught us again of an ancient history that was unknown to newcomers like me.

This land had not always been a prairie of moisture-rich, nutrient-dense soil that is perfect for growing crops and raising herds. For thousands of years, it had been a shallow yet diverse ecosystem of ducks, sturgeon, salmon, freshwater mussels, and millions of other creatures, all living together on what was once known as Sumas Lake. But tragically, Sumas Lake eventually became Sumas Prairie, when colonizers came to reclaim the land for the purpose of farming, buying up parcels of land to create intergenerational wealth that is still being passed down to those who call this region their home today. In his book *Before We Lost the Lake: A Natural and Human History of Sumas Valley*, local historian Chad Reimer outlines the ways that colonization, white immigrant farmers, nonnative animals and agricultural crops, and an intentional campaign to drain the original lake created not only a climate crisis but also a human rights crisis. The local Indigenous peoples—the Stó:lō people, or people of the river—lost the lake that their way of life was built around and that 85 percent of their traditional diet came from.

Acres were sold to incoming farmers for $60 to $120 per parcel as the landscape shifted from a thriving land to a drained river valley between 1920 and 1924. The Indigenous peoples who had lived here since time immemorial now had nowhere to go, as they lost their homes and way of life that was built around their relationship with the lake, recognizing when the lake would flood each year. They were forced to leave behind their homes that had been built on stilts to accommodate the earth's natural rhythms, rather than seeking to control them as the settlers had. The desire to harness and control, rather than nurture intimate relationships, is one of the biggest differences that I see between an Indigenous worldview and a colonized worldview. This pattern is reflected all over the world as colonization has altered the natural way of relating to the earth and her beings. There is no doubt in my mind that our current climate crisis is a direct result of colonization and the broken relationships we hold with the earth, each other, and our own bodies.

Climate change, flooding, loss of biodiversity, and other natural devastation comes when we see the earth as something to have dominion over rather than relationship with. Dominion, meaning to master or rule over, has been used by the British Empire to describe their colonies or territorial possessions. Canada's official motto, etched into the heavy stone of the Peace Tower on our Parliament buildings, reads, *A mari usque ad mare*. This comes from Psalm 72:8 in the Bible: "He shall also have dominion from sea to sea, and from the river unto the ends of the earth." With the mindset of colonization, humans have embodied this phrase of mastery and rule, regardless of which empire we come from. From the US's manifest destiny, the Roman Empire's conquest, Genghis Khan's Mongolian expansion, or the fact that, still today, the sun never sets on the British empire: everywhere that the mindset of dominion and colonization has reached, there has been death, destruction, and disembodiment. When we rise to social, political, and economic power, we forget the covenant of reciprocity that is embedded within our bodies and critical for the balance of interconnectedness within all things. We need only look at the coming climate catastrophe to see that our current ways of being, built on patriarchy, colonization, and white supremacy are directly responsible for the earth no longer being able to sustain us. We have used colonization to deploy the patriarchal approach of power *over* rather than the egalitarian value of power *with*, to dictate our relationships with our bodies, the land, and one another. When we cast aside this colonial way of thinking, we can return to the wisdom within our own bodies that sees humanity as a force to not rule over nature but rather be in relationship with it, as we are part of nature ourselves. This is why the practice of embodiment is inherently an act of decolonizing work. We reclaim every original, authentic, embodied part of ourselves as we reclaim everything that was stolen through the violence of colonization. This act of taking what does not belong to us without the covenant of reciprocity, without right relationship, is not only an act of colonization from centuries ago that established the world as we know it today; if we are not careful, it is also a mindset that is still deeply embedded into our collective psyche here in the Western world today.

To partake in their redistribution and rebranding without a reverence for and relationship with the cultures, traditions, and spirituality that they come from is cultural appropriation and a modern-day act of colonization. Western seekers who are looking for a deeper-rooted relationship to right ancestral traditions may seem innocent and harmless; but when not done in the right way, with respect and reciprocity, their search can do deep harm to communities of color who have already suffered greatly at the hands of Western colonialism, prejudice, violence, and racism. This is not to say that these particular traditions or others can't be accessed widely by all; rather, we each ought to sit with the wisdom of our bodies in self-reflection and ask ourselves if reciprocity is at the core of our relationships with these medicines, fashions, movements, and spiritual practices. We need to ensure that we are giving back to each relationship more than we are taking from them, so that we can be in right relationship with all. It is a small thing, but deeply profound, and it has the ability to change everything in the world. One of the reclaimed truths that I have learned through this practice is not to overlook the small things, for even in their smallness, there is great influence and power to be had.

The Parallels of Interconnectedness in Nature and in Community

When it comes to having one another's back, I've seen the single mothers' community do this better than anyone else I know. If you're fleeing an abusive home and need to start over with nothing, it is your fellow single moms who will give from the little they have to ensure that you have what you need to make ends meet. If you need someone to babysit, do a grocery store run for your sick child, add as an emergency contact for school, help with carpool, provide a safe place to regulate after a verbal attack from your abusive ex, or even deliver a cup of milk for your toddler's bottle in the middle of the night: you can rest assured that there is a single mom in your call history or internet group who will be there to get you through. The fundamentalist Christian church that I was raised in viewed single moms as sinners who made poor choices out of wedlock, and the political party I once voted for saw single moms as burdens on society who weighed down the federal budget. But I'll tell you this from my own lived experience: it was my unexpected years living as a single mother of two young children that showed me a community embodying more of the early church's precolonial resolve to love one another and provide for each other such that no one among them had any need. It was not the church or the federal government who did that; it was my fellow single moms.

In my single mom community, I proudly go by the title of "Auntie Tara." Everyone's kids refer to me as such, and I don't think they know, or even care, if I'm blood related to them or not. But perhaps it does not matter; the way we embraced one another and depended on one another for economic and emotional survival meant that we might as well have been blood related anyway. Likewise, in BIPOC communities, we often refer to our elders as Uncle or Auntie, because we know what it means to think collectively rather than individually. Beyond community survival, the honorifics of Uncle or Aunt demonstrate respect. No one goes by "Mister" or "Mrs." in our communities—that would be a far too impersonal way to address someone who would not hesitate to give you the shirt off their back if ever you needed something that they were able to give. Literally, I have walked out of the home of dear family friends wearing the very socks of my "uncle" from Borneo, who took them off his own feet to give them to me as a child. This way of communal living runs deep in our blood and shows up symbolically in our cultural rituals: from the Chun Hup "Tray of Togetherness" during Lunar New Year, to the ways that our children are raised together and, when necessary, scolded by any auntie in proximity, regardless of which child belongs to who. Likewise, when my community gets together, I don't care if it's your kids, his kids, her kids, or their kids: if kids are underfoot, I will feed them, care for them, and when necessary, teach them right from wrong through communal parenting. This is Big Auntie Energy, and every person in the BIPOC community knows exactly what I'm talking about. Aunties have quite a bit of notoriety in our communities, and everyone has an auntie in their life with an opinion on one thing or another. But no matter how nosy our aunties may be, we can always count on them to be there to bail us out when we need it!

This way of living defies the societal norms that center the heteronormative nuclear family of two parents and their children, living under one roof in a single-family home. BIPOC families and single-mother households commonly have more than one generation under one roof and sometimes prioritize chosen family over blood relatives, especially in the queer families who know what it means to depend on one another for survival outside of the patriarchal and colonial system. As I mentioned earlier, at one point my own family had four generations living under one roof, and while it was an intricate dance to manage all the family dynamics (and intergenerational trauma) that often clashed in various ways, I'm so grateful for the gift that that season of intergenerational co-living gave to my children. Perhaps the BIPOC, queer, and single-mother communities can invite into a reimaging of the future in the same way that mushrooms invite us into a richer understanding of symbiotic living and sustainability. Decolonizing my parenting and returning to my cultural roots has been an important part of my embodiment journey, because it is my ancestors' DNA that still pulses through my veins. To do this I had to unlearn the lies of patriarchy, colonization, and white supremacy while embracing not only my own full, authentic self but also a compassionate and grace-filled view of the "other" or those who are different than me. To do this effectively, we must reclaim our humanity through right relationship with all things. It starts with our own bodies and creates ripples outward.

Reclaiming Right Relationship in the Midst of Human Conflict

To be human is to be messy and to do harm. This does not justify our actions or behavior when we inflict harm on others, but it is realistic of the human experience. Conflict is, unfortunately, a part of every single relationship that exists on earth; to believe that there are no conflicts within nature would be an oversimplified way of looking at the nature of things. Animals fight, plants push against one another for sunlight, asteroids crash, and sometimes humans clash with one another too. Even the healthiest relationships will encounter conflict at some point. The goal is not to erase all conflicts from our lives but rather to navigate them in such a way that we remember the covenant of reciprocity that exists between us rather than resorting to violence and harm that dehumanizes those who we disagree with or who do us wrong.

When we approach conflict by seeking to be right, we lose immediately. The goal can never be to be right or to win; the goal must be to seek better understanding. To come to the table together, we mutually consent to accountability in relationship and to seeing humanity in one another's eyes. I know from personal, painful lived experience that this way of seeking conflict resolution is so very, very hard! In our pain and our wounding, we sometimes hunger and thirst for justice—and often this looks like punitive justice. We want to see the individual or institution who did us harm to receive retribution for their actions. We want to be validated. We want them to "get what's theirs." But if we harbor that kind of hatred and wounding, it will poison us from the inside out. We cannot make the other side come to the table to seek peace. We cannot control the actions of someone else. We cannot make anyone become a better person. Everyone is on their own healing journey, with their own lessons to learn and their own timeline. And the sad reality is that some people will never choose to reflect on the ways in which they have done us harm. All we can do is work through the things that we ourselves are directly responsible for, to dismantle our own ego and humanize all the parts of ourselves that we seek to re-embody and heal. It is an inside job.

For these reasons, calling people out from a distance will never work; we must call people into right relationship as they are willing.

Seeing others as the villain is not only dehumanizing but shuts down any real possibility for growth, understanding, accountability, and reconciliation. Plus, it's a very binary and colonial way of thinking. Do people harm others? Yes. Of course. As we have already discussed there is no one among us who has not been harmed and also done harm. But villainizing one another is not the way we heal or seek justice. Through a western lens, we are raised to believe that we are independent and to value self-resiliency. But our rights and desires cannot dominate over everything else. We can, and must, learn to do better if we want right relationship. A Mayan idea, captured by Chicano playwright Luis Valdez in his poem "Pensamiento Serpentino," says that "tú eres mi otro yo," which roughly translates to "you are my other me."

We must remember that we belong in relationship, with responsibilities to one another. Even though it is through our relationships that we can experience hurt, it is also through our relationships that we can experience healing. When we are harmed in community, there is a natural tendency to want to draw back from others or to put up our shields and prepare to fight the one who hurt us. But we must remember that it is also in community that we heal. We need spaces where we can be safe enough to be vulnerable and speak about all the ways that we have been hurt and also all the ways we have done harm. To make space for this repair, we need to view ourselves and our fellow humans with curiosity rather than condemnation. We need to believe that humans are inherently good but often lash out when our nervous system has been impacted by the effects of trauma. This radical act of looking for our goodness while witnessing one another in our fullness allows us to be seen, heard, known, and loved. When we do this for one another, we are able to see the impact of our actions. Without that, we leave space for shame to grow, and the rupture between us ignites a fortification of our defensive walls, protecting us so that we do not get hurt. But if we feel safe enough to come back together, and if we feel truly held in community, then it is possible for us to sit in the discomfort of that rupture and find our way back together again, even after we have messed up. This kind of compassionate accountability is the way we usher in transformation and allow our mistakes to lead the way toward greater understanding.

Sometimes, even when we have taken all the intentional steps to set up an environment for reconciliation and repair, the rupture will remain in our relationships. I've felt the pain of this before, and it still breaks my heart to think of friendships that have been lost because of our inability to come back to the table and talk it out. In some cases, I was not emotionally mature enough to see through my own trauma or shadow self, and in other occasions our inability to repair had nothing to do with me. Regardless, there are sometimes situations where you cannot make another person take accountability for the harm they caused, no matter how much we might like them to. In these situations we often need to establish embodied boundaries by distancing ourselves from the source of harm without dehumanizing the person doing harm.

When this happens, we can choose to remove ourselves and no longer participate in the harmful behaviors that are taking place. If the person causing the harm is receiving social power and attention for causing harm to others, we disrupt this cycle of abuse by removing ourselves and removing the social power that they are receiving from our presence. Doing this in a way that does not villainize, dehumanize, or "cancel" the other person is an essential factor to respecting the inherent dignity that belongs to every living being. And this is of the utmost importance when there is a rupture in a relationship.

We must protect the vulnerable but also not attack or shame the person who has done harm. Instead we must focus our calls for accountability toward the behavior, ideologies, and institutions that are doing harm. There is a significant difference. By directing our calls for justice in this way, we focus on a true source of harm while making space for the perpetrator to learn from their mistakes with the possibility of restoration back into right relationship. This way of healing relationships is countercultural to the punitive justice system that has been established in North America and almost everywhere else around the world. We've been conditioned to view punishment, isolation, and dehumanization as justified retribution when harm has been caused. But in our interpersonal relationships, having the emotional maturity to somatically process our pain in a way that does not villainize others provides a transformative view of justice that leaves the door open for the possibility of growth and change.

To be in right relationship, while the forces of commodification and oppression seek to pull us apart, is a powerful revolution. All the division, disconnection, and disembodiment that is happening within our bodies is also happening in the world around us. We must never lose sight of our humanity—either within ourselves or within others—because once we do, we all lose. When we return to embodiment, we come home to the truth about our bodies: that they are wholly good, miraculous, and wonderful; that there is divine mystery that dwells beneath our skin; that the forces of body-based oppression and hierarchy can never stamp out the still, small voice of truth that lives inside us. When we remember this and live it out in our bodies, we wield a profound weapon against anything that seeks to commodify or control our bodies.

Once we begin to learn how to view our own humanity again and give space for the messiness that is humanity, then we can see others by the same framework as well. This helps us humanize one another and move out of the violent cycles of body-based oppression, power hierarchies, and punitive justice. Without remembering our humanity and the somatic skills of recognizing the ways that shame, outrage, anger, and trauma ignite reactionary responses within us, we will not be able to progress forward as a society. We must remember our interconnectedness. For this reason, I caution myself and everyone else around us that we must pay attention to what we use to justify and harbor our hate. This is key. What we use to justify our anger and hate is what we use to justify our dehumanization of one another and perpetuate the cycle of harm. This is the foundation of all broken relationships; we forget that we belong to one another, we forget our interconnectedness and the convent of reciprocity that we must share for there to be mutual flourishing. This is the only way to truly transform systems of body-based oppression. It must start from within; it must begin and end with relationship.

Institutionalizing Nonviolence and Right Relationship

Likewise, when we are seeking to dismantle and rebuild the political, economic, and social systems of body-based oppression, we must rebuild with right relationship in our minds. As violence and division have been institutionalized through the systems of our society and refined over time, we must bravely step into a new paradigm of relating to one another by looking at humanity through the common lens of embodiment and calling in the best of who we are as a species. It is not enough to dismantle and confront what is wrong in the world; we must also multiply what is right. To do so, I feel the wisdom of my somatic body, I look at the parallels of symbiotic living in the natural world, and I seek out the guidance of great teachers who have paved the way before. Teachings of transformational justice, truth and reconciliation, interconnectedness, and nonviolence are all radically different approaches to creating a world with less harm, more embodiment, and more justice.

I see these teachings embodied in the grandmas I know who create the backbone of our communities, who steam bao, steep tea, and stir the resistance from kitchens all across the world. I see this embodied in the life of Jesus of Nazareth as he taught us to break bread with our enemies and step back from throwing the first stone of condemnation. I see this in the radically different way of organizing movements according to Dr. Martin Luther King Jr.'s nonviolence philosophy, an approach to nonviolent conflict resolution. If our society has been structured around the patriarchal, white supremacist, colonial framework of violence, othering, power, and prejudice, could we likewise rebuild a new structure around centering our collective humanity and remembering the covenant of reciprocity? Kingian nonviolence trainer Kazu Haga asks, "What aspects of human nature do our institutions nurture?" It's a valid question. If militarization, ableism, colorism, misogyny, homophobia, and racism can be all institutionalized, as they have, can we not also institutionalize nonviolence, interconnectedness, embodiment, and transformational justice? I deeply believe we can. I see this in the way that Indigenous and Asian cultural teachings and protocols create the foundation for interconnected community relationships. We can begin in our own bodies and extend out to share these teachings with our families, our schools, our community groups, and our institutions. We can build schools, hospitals, prisons, churches, universities, midwifery centers, and sports academies on the foundational teachings of conflict reconciliation, deescalation, somatic literacy, antiracism, decolonization, and trauma-informed practices. This will require more than a two-hour or one-day workshop. This new way of viewing humanity and relationships must replace the old curriculum and programming that we are raised on and shift into a new way of being.

A New Approach for Embodied Living

Years ago, I made this conscious choice to shift the way I raised my children and remove punitive correction from my parenting. As someone who grew up in both a culturally Asian home and a conservative Christian home, my childhood was very strict. Corporal punishment (i.e., spanking) was very common. In my early years as a parent, I leaned heavily on the way I had been raised as a blueprint for how I would raise my own children. But every time I approached my sweet babies in this matter, something within me broke. The somatic sensations within my own body were continuously telling me that I would not teach them to turn away from violence by inflicting violence on them as a deterrent. This was not the way to teach my children to be better. Instead of watching them rise to make better choices with their words and actions, I witnessed them shrinking down in trauma and fear, often resorting to lying or throwing their siblings under the bus to escape the pain and punishment themselves. Is that what I wanted them to become? Was the aggressor who I wanted to become? The answer in my body was an unwavering no.

So I attempted a new approach. I didn't read books on gentle parenting or study alternative forms of discipline; rather, I trusted the inner compass of my own embodied wisdom and sat with them in their struggle and their big feelings to try to understand what had caused them to lash out in a way that inflicted harm on those around them. The results were instantly visible. Of course, there were times when they still chose wrong and needed to be corrected, but every time we sat together and worked it out, we found our way back to one another in mutual understanding. Sometimes this process was long and took hours of sitting in the car, the grocery store, the parking lot, or on the kitchen floor. Often there were tears, tantrums, and even silent shutdowns. We missed or were late for many, many different appointments and playdates because I chose to walk the long, winding path of nonviolence and reconciliation. But in the end, it made space for something within each of us that was far more valuable than an obedient child. We made room for deescalation, somatic experiencing, and a safe place to learn and grow. It was important for them to know that they always belonged and there was nothing they could possibly do that would push them away from me. Were there still consequences to actions? Yes, life offered many natural consequences. But instead of deploying a system of discipline and punishment built on violence and punitive justice, I chose the path of listening to why my children chose to do what they did so that we could correct the issue at the root of the problem, rather than giving it space to manifest and grow into bigger, uglier behaviors later on.

Whether through parenting or community work, shame is rarely a motivator for us to do better. When we treat one another as bad, we often inadvertently create the environment for those shame-filled messages to become internalized, like a self-fulfilling prophecy that pushes us away from one another and ourselves. When shame is present, we will hide the misunderstood pieces of ourselves and push them into exile. We become disembodied and fragmented, which in turn pushes our collective society to becoming disembodied and fragmented. But it doesn't have to be this way. Recognizing the habitual responses that we carry in our bodies gives us the opportunity to change them and turn to a new way of being human and more humane. It is possible to practically live in alignment with the urgings that can be felt deep within our bodies as we long for something more. The revolution starts within.

Reflection

Human relationships:

* Are there interpersonal relationships in my life that are in need of healing?

* Am I safe enough to show up in my relationships as my most authentic, embodied self?

* Am I making space for others in my relationships to show up safely as their most authentic, embodied self?

* If no, what can I do to be in right relationship with these people? Am I able to ethically and compassionately hold others accountable for any harm that has been done between us? Am I able to ethically and compassionately hold myself accountable for any harm that I am responsible for?

* How can I embody repair, reconciliation, and reintegration of my relationships after a rupture? How do I reaffirm to those who have wronged me that I still believe in their goodness and their ability to learn and grow?

* Do I need to establish embodied boundaries as an act of self-care, apart from someone who is refusing to learn from their mistakes?

Nonhuman relationships:

With the earth and nonhuman kin:

* Do I have a reciprocal relationship with earth? If yes, how can I deepen my relationship with the earth?

* If not, how can I repair and heal my relationship with the earth to bring more reverence and understanding with the nonhuman world?

With institutions and ideologies:

* Are the ideologies that I hold or the institutions that I am a part of doing harm or bringing healing to myself and others? Is body-based oppression present in the ideologies and institutions that I am a part of?

* Are these ideologies and institutions making more safe space for myself and others to be our most authentic, embodied selves?

* How can I reimagine the ideologies and institutions that I am apart of in order to ensure that there is mutual flourishing and reciprocity for all?

* Do I need to deconstruct my ideologies and institutions in order to ensure that there is mutual flourishing and reciprocity for all?

Invitation

Healing our relationships with each other and the earth begins with establishing a deeper knowing and understanding of one another. We do this by listening and spending time with those who we wish to build a deeper relationship with.

Spend more time within nature. Wiggle your toes into the dirt. Lie with your back on the ground, looking up at the sky and taking big, deep belly breaths. Soak your body in the water. Notice how your body feels when you are closer to nature. Spend time becoming more familiar with the forests, fields, and shorelines near where you live. Learn about the animals, the nonhuman kin, that you share these spaces with. What are their life cycles like? What do they depend on for survival? When we take from the earth, who is impacted? And how can we enter into these spaces with a relationship of reciprocity, ensuring the mutual flourishing of all?

Look around you and see who lives in your neighborhood. Are there people or community groups who are different from you culturally, economically, or politically? Are there stereotypes or assumptions that you may have about those people? If it is safe enough, reach out, without expectation or agenda, to build a relationship with these people around you. This will not happen overnight. Aim to establish an authentic human connection, built on the foundation of mutual flourishing and genuine understanding. You may be surprised with how much you have to learn from those who are different from you. How does your relationship with them shift your ideologies and perhaps, even the institutions that you belong to? Only when we can see and embrace the humanity within one another can we heal the relationship we have with one another in this world.

Acknowledgments

It took a village to bring this book to life. There are so many incredible teachers, friends, family, coconspirators, mentors, rebels, and trailblazers who collectively played a role in making this book possible. The words on these pages are the outpouring of everything these revolutionary humans have nurtured within me that now gets to spill over and be shared with the world.

This book was written on the unceded traditional territories of the Kwantlen, Katzie, Matsqui, and Semiahmoo First Nations. I am humbled to be a guest on these lands, to learn from the cedars, be held by the Stó:lō river (Fraser River), and play with my toes in the soil. You have generously welcomed me to be nourished here and find my place among you. May this book be an invitation for us to find our way back to the land, and into right relationship and reciprocity with one another.

To my parents, thank you for listening as I wrote the hard things. You have both gone around the world for me multiple times and I know, deep in my bones, that you always did your best for me with what you had in each moment.

Mom, you knew I was meant to write a book before anyone else in the world. While these pages may not have been the words you imagined me writing, I am grateful nonetheless for the seed you planted over ten years ago. Thank you for giving me the space to honestly share my story from my perspective and for loving me through every stage of life as I have evolved.

Dad, thank you for the years we spent discussing theology and biblical interpretation over root beer floats and around the kitchen table. We may have diverged to arrive at different places in our spirituality, but I'm grateful we've found a way to stay connected through it all. Thank you for loving me even when you didn't understand me.

My precious babies, Chayton, Skyana, and Satori: thank you for your patience with me throughout the years it took to write this book and for sharing your mom so that I could do this work. You are a beautiful reminder of why this book is needed, and I pray you will find your true self and embody liberation always. Mama loves you and I'll be cheering you on in your corner forever.

My love, Anthony: where do I even begin? I am so grateful that we found our way back to each other after so many years. You have been my greatest cheerleader and teammate through this process. I love cocreating this life with you. Thank you for being my safe harbor, for inviting me to live more honestly, for bringing breakfast to my writing desk, and for doing more than 50 percent at times so I could bring this vision to life. I could write endless words on how you loved me and helped me melt my walls so that I could come back to life. Our former selves would be in awe to see where we are now and the battles we have fought to get here. Every day I am grateful you exist.

Henry, you are the best boy in the world! Thank you for all the cuddles and for keeping my toes warm while I wrote.

To Trinity McFadden and Alex Field of The Bindery, thank you for taking a chance on me. You had my back every step of the way. I am honored to have you on my team, believing in this book and helping me birth it. The wisdom and insight that you brought to this process was invaluable.

I'm so grateful to my amazing editor Lisa Kloskin and the entire team at Broadleaf Books. Thank you for championing my book and bringing it to shelves everywhere. Broadleaf was the perfect home and family of voices for my book to live with. Thank you for the important stories you are bringing to the world.

Elisabeth Ivey, your keen eye and wise insights made this book far better than it would have been on my own. You knew exactly where to challenge me to dig deeper and how to remind me of the magic that is possible. Thank you for saying *yes* to joining this project.

Janay Nachel, you brought my vision to life and found a way to make us all feel seen through your beautiful cover art. Thank you.

Josh Harris, you gave me the push I needed to get my feet off the ledge. Thank you for seeing what my words could offer and for helping me find the courage to unleash them.

Jessica Birak and Mel Pederson, thank you for your fierce friendship. You've seen me at my worst and loved me through all of it. I would not be the woman I am today if it were not for the unconditional ways that you have held me, inspired me, and celebrated when I embody my most authentic self.

Shadae Johnson-Jensen, you are my sister. Thank you for sharing your wisdom with me and for embodying what it looks like to live in right relationship with all things. You are so precious to me.

Christina Wiebe (née Wong), Lee Henning, and Istredd Cheng, having your beautiful collaboration on this project has added so much. We are the chorus of voices reimagining how we exist in the world and the liberation we can achieve for our bodies. Thank you for entrusting me to share your stories.

To my Miss BC family, the SheLoves Community, One TWU, and the Institute for Somatic Sex Education, being part of these communities and witnessing the brave way every one of you shows up each day has inspired me to do the same. May we continue to love one another well as we rebuild a more inclusive, just, and safe world for all.

To Crystal Sing Giles, Idelette McVicker, Shaley Hoogendoorn, Matt Schell, Olivia Wong, Casey Desjarlais, Dakota Bear, Jamie Lee Finch, Morgan Day Cecil, Sophia Johnson, Lauren Deleary, Kevin Garcia, Mattias Roberts, Christy Bauman, Cheryl Bear, Nicolle Hodges, Valerie Rein, Brittany Graves, Brenda Marie Davies, Megan Tschantz, Hillary McBride, Kai Cheng Thom, Michelle Li, and Katya Nova: our conversations have expanded my thinking, influenced my writing, and made me a better human. I'm honored to know you all.

To Richard Rohr, Austin Channing Brown, Kazu Haga, Robin Wall Kimmerer, Resmaa Menakem, Lilla Watson, Glennon Doyle, Jonathan Van Ness, Adrienne Maree Brown, Sonya Renee Taylor, Ev'Yan Whitney, Leah Lakshmi, Gabor Maté, Brené Brown, Kimberly Ann Johnson, Stephen Porges, Staci Hanes, Peter Levine, Rev. René August, Lisa Sharon Harper, Shane Claiborne, Richard Twiss, Regena Thomashauer, and the many others who have taught me throughout the years. Your work means so much to me. Listening and learning from you has created a ripple effect that I, and many others, have benefited from. Thank you for bravely showing us how to live beyond the status quo.

To the social movements of Women's Liberation, LGBTQ2S+ rights, Civil Rights, Occupy, Black Lives Matter, Me Too, Idle No More, Land Back, and Stop Asian Hate: I was raised on your example and have benefited so greatly from your sacrifices. Thank you for showing me the significance of grassroots community activism and how we speak truth to power. I am indebted to your sacrifices.

To my clients, my online community, and the community of Reclamation Circles, it is an honor to witness your big, brave lives. I have held each of your stories in my heart while writing this book.

You show me what is possible when we come back into loving relationship with our bodies and heal our relationships with one another. You are the magic.

And finally, to my precious body—none of this would be possible without you. We make an incredible team, and I am grateful for all the wisdom you share with me every day. Thank you for being my ally and allowing me to experience all the goodness that this life has to offer.

Notes

Introduction

"in which we live": Staci Hanes, *The Politics of Trauma: Somatics, Healing, and Social Justice,* read by Julie Slater (Berkeley, CA: North Atlantic Books, 2019), audiobook, 14 hr., 40 min.

Reclamation

we simply hand each other the matches: From a conversation with Dr. Valerie Rein.

Two-Spirit: Sue-Ellen Jacobs, Wesley Thomas, and Sabine Lang, *Two-Spirit People: Native American Gender Identity, Sexuality, and Spirituality* (Urbana: University of Illinois Press, 1997).

Shaking Off Shame

"body equals tomb": Christian Irigaray, "Soma Sema: The Body as a Prison for the Soul," Academia.edu, n.d., accessed May 17, 2022, https://www.academia.edu/33117741/Soma_Sema_The_Body_as_a_Prison_for_the_Soul.

"when what happened to you was happening": The Wisdom of Trauma website, n.d., accessed May 26, 2022, https://hub.wisdomoftrauma.com.

to our true selves: Robin Wall Kimmerer, *Braiding Sweetgrass: Indigenous Wisdom, Scientific Knowledge, and the Teachings of Plants* (Minneapolis: Milkweed Editions, 2015).

Emotional Expression, Not Repression

in the Emotion Code: Bradley Nelson, *The Emotion Code: How to Release Your Trapped Emotions for Abundant Health, Love, and Happiness* (New York: St. Martin's Essentials, 2019).

2013 study: Benjamin P. Chapman, Kevin Fiscella, Ichiro Kawachi, Paul Duberstein, and Peter Muennig, "Emotion Suppression and Mortality Risk over a 12-Year Follow-Up," *Journal of Psychosomatic Research* 75, no. 4 (2013): 381–85, https://doi.org/10.1016/j.jpsychores.2013.07.014.

understanding and diagnosis: Laura Kiesel, "Women and Pain: Disparities in Experience and Treatment," *Harvard Health Blog*, October 9, 2017, https://www.health.harvard.edu/blog/women-and-pain-disparities-in-experience-and-treatment-2017100912562; Camille Noe Pagán, "When Doctors Downplay Women's Health Concerns," *New York Times*, May 3, 2018, https://www.nytimes.com/2018/05/03/well/live/when-doctors-downplay-womens-health-concerns.html; Mary Beth Flanders-Stepans, "Birthing Briefs: Alarming Racial Differences in Maternal Mortality," *Journal of Perinatal Education* 9, no. 2 (2000): 50–51, https://doi.org/10.1624/105812400x87653.

the intake documents: Katherine Pouba and Ashley Tianen, "Lunacy in the 19th Century: Women's Admission to Asylums in United States of America." *Oshkosh Scholar* 1, April 2006, https://minds.wisconsin.edu/bitstream/handle/1793/6687/Lunacy%20in%20the%2019th%20Century.pdf?sequence=1.

many cultural influences: David D. Gilmore, *Manhood in the Making: Cultural Concepts of Masculinity* (New Haven, CT: Yale University Press, 1990).

Manliness of Christ: Thomas Hughes, *The Manliness of Christ* (Cambridge, MA: H. Altemus, 1896).

a study: Katharina Gapp, Ali Jawaid, Peter Sarkies, Johannes Bohacek, Pawel Pelczar, Julien Prados, Laurent Farinelli, Eric Miska, and Isabelle M. Mansuy, "Implication of Sperm RNAs in Transgenerational Inheritance of the Effects of Early Trauma in Mice," *Nature Neuroscience*

17, no. 5 (2014): 667–69, https://doi.org/10.1038/nn.3695; Arielle Duhaime-Ross, "Sperm Can Pass Trauma Symptoms through Generations, Study Finds," *The Verge*, April 13, 2014, https://www.theverge.com/2014/4/13/5606070/sperm-pass-trauma-symptoms-through-generations; Martha Henriques, "Can the Legacy of Trauma Be Passed Down the Generations?" BBC Future, March 26, 2019, https://www.bbc.com/future/article/20190326-what-is-epigenetics.

700 percent: Johna Baylon and Leyland Cecco, "Attacks Make Vancouver 'Anti-Asian Hate Crime Capital of North America,'" *The Guardian*, May 23, 2021, https://www.theguardian.com/world/2021/may/23/vancoucer-anti-asian-hate-crimes-increase.

Healing Trauma

a client of mine, Mary: This story, and the others told in the book, are shared with permission. Names and details have been changed to protect anonymity.

fawn response: For more on the idea of the fawn response, see Pete Walker, *Complex PTSD: From Surviving to Thriving; A Guide and Map for Recovering from Childhood Trauma* (Lafayette, CA: Azure Coyote, 2013).

"human needs": Gabor Maté, The Wisdom of Trauma website, accessed May 26, 2022. https://hub.wisdomoftrauma.com.

adverse childhood experiences: Vincent J. Felitti, "The Relation between Adverse Childhood Experiences and Adult Health: Turning Gold into Lead," *Permanente Journal* 6, no. 1 (2002): 44–47, https://www.ncbi.nlm.nih.gov/pmc/articles/PMC6220625/.

Dr. Vincent Felitii: Vincent J. Felitti, Robert F. Anda, Dale Nordenberg, David F. Williamson, Alison M. Spitz, Valerie Edwards, Mary P. Koss, and James S. Marks, "Relationship of Childhood Abuse and Household Dysfunction to Many of the Leading Causes of Death in Adults," *American Journal of Preventive Medicine* 14, no. 4 (1998): 245–58, https://doi.org/10.1016/s0749-3797(98)00017-8.

Politics, Injustice, and the Body

My Grandmother's Hands: Resmaa Menakem, *My Grandmother's Hands: Racialized Trauma and the Pathway to Mending Our Hearts and Bodies,* read by Resmaa Menakem (Las Vegas, NV: Central Recovery Press, 2017), audiobook, 10 hr., 18 min.

Braiding Sweetgrass: Robin Wall Kimmerer, *Braiding Sweetgrass: Indigenous Wisdom, Scientific Knowledge and the Teachings of Plants,* read by Robin Wall Kimmerer (Minneapolis: Milkweed Editions, 2013), audiobook, 16 hr., 44 min.

a study conducted: Brenda L. Gunn, "Ignored to Death: Systemic Racism in the Canadian Healthcare System," submission to EMRIP the Study on Health, n.d., accessed January 30, 2022, https://www.ohchr.org/sites/default/files/Documents/Issues/IPeoples/EMRIP/Health/UniversityManitoba.pdf.

white bodies: Mary Beth Flanders-Stepans, "Birthing Briefs: Alarming Racial Differences in Maternal Mortality," *Journal of Perinatal Education* 9, no. 2 (2000): 50–51, https://doi.org/10.1624/105812400x87653.

John Marion Sims: Brynn Holland, "The 'Father of Modern Gynecology' Performed Shocking Experiments on Slaves," History, December 4, 2018, https://www.history.com/news/the-father-of-modern-gynecology-performed-shocking-experiments-on-slaves.

until very recently: Scott Jaschik, "Anger over Stereotypes in Textbook," Inside Higher Ed, October 23, 2017, https://www.insidehighered.com/news/2017/10/23/nursing-textbook-pulled-over-stereotypes.

"European civilisation": Marilyn French, *From Eve to Dawn: A History of Women,* vol. 2, *The Masculine Mystique* (New York: Feminist Press, 2008), 121.

religious systems' control: Rachel Reed, *Reclaiming Childbirth as a Rite of Passage: Weaving Ancient Wisdom with Modern Knowledge* (Yandina, QLD, Australia: Word Witch Press, 2021), 15.

"white community": "Jim Crow Laws," n.d., accessed January 31, 2022, https://www.gcsu.edu/sites/files/page-assets/node-2213/attachments/jim_crow_educational_resource_.pdf.

No One Left Behind

"ugly laws": Susan M. Schweik, *The Ugly Laws: Disability in Public* (New York: New York University Press, 2010).

"public view": Marcia Pearce Burgdorf and Robert Burgdorf Jr., *A History of Unequal Treatment: The Qualifications of Handicapped Persons as a 'Suspect Class' under the Equal Protection Clause*, 15 SANTA CLARA L. REV. 854, 863 (1975) (quoting CHICAGO, ILL. MUN. CODE §36-34 [1966]).

"difficulties and risks": Jacobus Tenbroek, "The Right to Live in the World: The Disabled in the Law of Torts," *California Law Review* 54, no. 2 (1969): 841–919.

Beyond the Binary

Ojibwe people: Harlan Pruden and Beverly Gorman, "LGBTQ2 Well-Being Education 'Two-Spirit People: Then and Now,'" 2014, accessed March 18, 2022, https://www.ihs.gov/sites/lgbt/themes/responsive2017/display_objects/documents/lgbttwospirithistory.pdf.

Langi tribe: Tomás Prower, *Queer Magic: LGBT+ Spirituality and Culture from around the World* (Woodbury, MN: Llewellyn Publications, 2018); Jessica L. Anderson, "Gender, Local Justice, and Ownership: Confronting Masculinities and Femininities in Northern Uganda," *Peace Research* 41, no. 2 (2009): 59–83.

Mbuti people: Colin M. Turnbull, *The Forest People* (London: Bodley Head, 2015).

largely a performance: Judith Butler, *Gender Trouble: Feminism and the Subversion of Identity* (New York: Routledge, 1990).

"and public offense": William N. Eskridge, *Gaylaw: Challenging the Apartheid of the Closet* (London: Harvard University Press, 2002).

Historian Christopher Adam Mitchell: Hugh Ryan, "How Dressing in Drag Was Labeled a Crime in the 20th Century," History, June 28, 2019,

https://www.history.com/news/stonewall-riots-lgbtq-drag-three
-article-rule.

Pleasure

four to six years old: National Child Traumatic Stress Network, "Sexual Development and Behavior in Children: Information for Parents and Caregivers," n.d., accessed February 18, 2022, https://www.nctsn.org /sites/default/files/resources/sexual_development_and_behavior_in _children.pdf.

in the last year: Jennifer Gunter, *The Vagina Bible* (New York: Little, Brown, 2019), 103–104.

the Erotic Blueprint: Miss Jaiya, "Erotic Blueprints and Breakthrough with Jaiya," Erotic Blueprint Breakthrough, n.d., accessed May 18, 2022, https://missjaiya.com.

In Right Relationship

between 1920 and 1924: Emma Smith and Katelyn Verstraten, "Sumas First Nation Seeks Compensation for Its Lost Lake," *Vancouver Sun,* May 6, 2013, https://vancouversun.com/news/sumas-first-nation-in-bc -canada-seeks-compensation-for-its-lost-lake-taken-90-years-ago.

flood each year: Michelle Gomez, "Sumas First Nation Built on Higher Ground, Unaffected by Flooding in Former Lake Bed, Says Chief," CBC, November 20, 2021, https://www.cbc.ca/news/canada/british -columbia/sumas-lake-history-1.6255693.

"do our institutions nurture?": Kazu Haga, Bernard Lafayette, and David C. Jehnsen, *Healing Resistance: A Radically Different Response to Harm,* read by Tom Parks (Berkeley, CA: Parallax Press, 2020), audiobook, 10 hr., 2 min.